IT in Primary Science

Roger Frost

*A compendium of ideas for
using computers and teaching science.*

IT in Primary Science ISBN 0-9520257-3-6

updating and replacing The IT in Primary Science Book
ISBN 0-9520257-0-1

Titles in this series:

The IT in Science Book of data logging and control, ISBN 0 9520257 1 X
The IT in Secondary Science Book, ISBN 0 9520257 2 8
Data logging in Practice, ISBN 0 9520257 4 4
Software for teaching science, ISBN 0 9520257 5 2

How to contact the publishers, our suppliers and the author

IT in Primary Science was written and produced by Roger Frost. It is published by and © of IT in Science, 7 Sutton Place, London E9 6EH Telephone or Fax: 0208 986 3526.
E-mail to books@rogerfrost.com

IT in science information is available via the Internet at: www.rogerfrost.com

Distributed by
The Association for Science Education (Booksales), College Lane, Hatfield, Herts. AL10 9AA. Telephone 01707 267411. Fax: 01707 266532

TTS, Monk Road, Alfreton, Derbyshire, D55 7RL Tel: 01773 830255 Fax: 01773 830325

Australia:
Southern Biological Services Pty. Ltd, 19-21 Worrell Street, Nunawading, Vic. 3131. Australia. Telephone: 03 98774597 Fax: 03 98942309

USA:
Fisher Education Tel: 1 800 955 1177 or www.fisheredu.com/

Data Harvest Educational Inc. 349 Lang Blvd, Grand Island, 14072.

Tel: 1 800 436 3062 or http://www.interlog.com/~easylog

New Zealand:
Education Advisory Services, Private Bag 92601, Symonds St, Auckland

Canada:
Data Harvest Educational Inc. 2671 Romark Mews, Mississauga, Ontario, L5L 2Z4.

Tel: 905 828 6166 Fax: 905 607 1525 or http://www.interlog.com/~easylog

Please address bookshop and enquiries for bulk purchases to the publisher

This edition ISBN 0 9520257 3 6 was first published September 1995. It was reprinted with new releases of software included within the text in Nov 1995, March 1996, July 1996, Dec 1996 Aug 1998, Jan 1999, June 1999, Sept 1999, Nov 1999
First published as The IT in Primary Science Book ISBN 0 9520257 2 8 1993
A catalogue record for this is available from the British Library
Graphics originated using Arts & Letters Graphic Editor and Micrografx Designer.
Printed by The Printing Centre, Store Street, London WI / Sackville Oak Ltd, Picadilly, London W1, UK

Acknowledgements

Thanks are due to the following for their valuable help and advice in their personal capacities. Their ideas and comments on the original manuscript were gratefully received and used to prepare this book:

Helen Taylor, primary IT advisory teacher, London Borough of Richmond
John Wardle, Microscope IT in Science centre, Sheffield Hallam University
Geoff Strack, London Borough of Hackney
Alan Ovenden, London Borough of Newham
Pat Strack & Bill Hodder of Training in Technology, London Borough of Haringey
Juliet Edmunds, South Thames College
Dr Angela MacFarlane, Homerton College
Trevor Millum and colleagues, Resource
Liz Singleton, Bradford LEA
Reprographic advice Ann Casey, Islington LEA
Special thanks to Esmé Glauert, Institute of Education, London
Edited by Rosie Kentish of Deep See Subs
Cover photograph by Len Cross Associates, with thanks to David Sayers (mouse trainer) and Copenhagen School, Islington

The stimulus for the ideas here came from material including:

IT in Science publications: The IT in Science Book of Data logging and Control (IT in Science)
The IT in Primary Science Book (IT in Science)
The IT in Secondary Science Book (IT in Science)
IT in Science Buff book (IT in Science)
National Council for Educational Technology publications:
Practical Science with Microcomputers (NCET)
Primary Science Investigations with IT (NCET)
Science Investigations and IT (NCET)
Supporting Science (NCET)
Sensing Science (NCET)
Science schemes and books:
Nelson Science (Nelson)
Nelson-Bath Science 5-16 (Nelson)
Roy Richardson's An Early Start series (Simon and Shuster)
Collins Primary Science, Spectrum Science (Collins Educational)

And also:

Creative ideas for using spreadsheets in science by Jane M Morris (Cleveland Educational Computing Centre)
Handling Data with Databases and Spreadsheets by Mike Hammond (Hodder & Stoughton)
Insight software applications guide (Leicester university / Longman Logotron)
Essex Spreadsheet Posters (Essex LEA)

About the author

Roger Frost was an analytical biochemist for ten years before joining teaching. In 1988 he became a science and IT advisory teacher for ILECC, the London computer centre and later for the North London Science Centre.
In 1993 he was appointed to the post of freelance writer, trainer and IT consultant. His published work includes:

Software for teaching science, ISBN 0 9520257 5 2
Data logging in practice, ISBN 0 9520257 4 4
IT in Primary Science - Dutch edition (CPS, Holland) 1995
The IT in Secondary Science Book 1994 ISBN 0 9520257 2 8
The IT in Science Book of data logging and control (IT in Science), 1993 ISBN 0 9520257 1 X
Enhancing Science with IT (NCET) 1994 co-author ISBN 1 85379270 5
Information Technology (Nelson), 1993 co-author ISBN 0 17438572 2
The IT in Primary Science Book (IT in Science), 1993 ISBN 0 9520257 0 1 Out of Print
The IT in Science Blue book, (IT in Science), 1992 Out of print
The IT in Science Buff book, (IT in Science), 1991 Out of print

Contents

Quick overview

This book is a catalogue of ideas for teaching science using information technology.

How information technology helps scientists

Prepare experiment plans, reports, letters, instruction sheets and questionaires.

Word processor

Assemble drawings, diagrams, photos and words on a page.

Graphics and DTP

Scientists need to do many things which IT can help with ...

We need to communicate

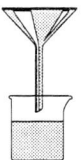

We need to measure

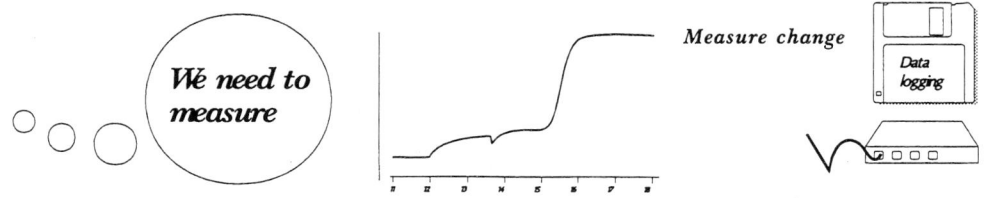

Measure change

Data logging

We need to handle and analyse data

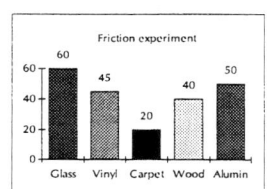

Organise, store and analyse survey results

Database program

Store and analyse records kept in a table.

Spreadsheet program

We need to model our ideas

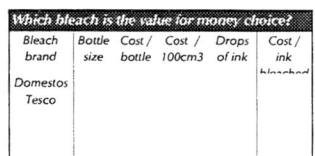

Which bleach is the value for money choice?

Bleach brand	Bottle size	Cost / bottle	Cost / 100cm3	Drops of ink	Cost / ink bleached
Domestos					
Tesco					

Draw graphs and create mathematical models to test our ideas.

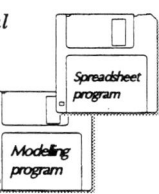
Spreadsheet program

Modeling program

Calculate and predict

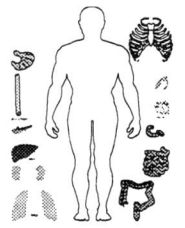

Create diagrams to see if our ideas will work. See how things fit together.

Graphics program

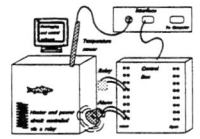

Create working systems to see how things work. See if our own ideas will work.

Measure & Control

Preface

How information technology helps scientists

Scientists need to measure and communicate, to handle information and model ideas. In essence, they need to process information. Young scientists have similar needs - as they do science work they write, draw graphs, do maths and make measurements - so they too process information.

The technology for processing information includes tools such as the word processor, the spreadsheet, database programs, sensors, and modelling programs. Database programs allow us to search for information and look to patterns within it. Sensors help us to measure changes and draw graphs. Modelling programs help us present scientific ideas that are too hard to get a grip on in real life. Spreadsheet programs take the strain of making tables, drawing graphs and working with numbers. If there is a common thread here, it's that these tools allow us to do more and go further.

It is important that children see how today's scientist works. It is important that they be equipped for the technology-rich world in which they live. It's also important, a legal requirement even, that they use information technology.

But when teachers started using the technology in class, other advantages became apparent. When their pupils became fluent in using sensors, the computer offered a new insight into science: they gained something that helped them to understand and encouraged them to explore. When the children used databases and spreadsheets they didn't just draw graphs, they could go on to interpret them. And when they worked together with a word processor, they started talking with zeal, not the usual gossip, but about science. Children who were challenged by doing things 'the old way' were able to move on. The tools that started life as information processing tools became really special tools to enhance our teaching. These were tools for the mind.

And for all the speed of computers, I doubt if anyone saved any time. What was saved - by not having to draw tables, or colour-in graphs, or 'write it out neatly' or take thermometer readings - was spent straight away, examining the science that had started to open up. In the search for more science, this book shows where information technology can be exploited and add value to our science teaching.

Roger Frost

A programme of study

This section is a list of the kinds of things children might do using IT in their science work. It is the framework for the ideas which you will find detailed throughout this book.

Science and IT from 5 to 7 years

Children use IT to present their work. They might use a word processor to produce a caption for a picture. They can progress on to write a sentence or a basic report of their investigation. Children may need help with the keyboard: you might get a helper to do the typing or use a Concept (or overlay) keyboard. You might stick lower case letters on a standard keyboard. They should use the computer for drafting work - rather than copying up handwritten work. Children should store their work on disk and develop it further on a later occasion.

Children might classify things with graphics programs which allow them to rearrange pictures with a mouse. They might use graphics programs or ready-made pictures to illustrate their work.

Children can browse a CD-ROM and find things out. They can use a word processor table to record their results. They can use pictogram or other easy graphing programs to prepare bar graphs from their results. Science adventure programs or CD-ROM will allow them to model aspects of science.

As an introduction to control they use LOGO, programmable toys, robots or video recorders. Later they might use sensors to find out 'which is hottest, which is loudest or which is brightest.'

Children learn to appreciate how others use the IT tools that they use.

Science and IT from 8 to 11 years

Children might use a word processor to produce a plan or a report of an investigation. They might then take such a report and develop it into a poster or a news story. They can use graphics programs and ready-made 'clip-art' to illustrate these.

Science programs or CD-ROM will allow children to interact with models of science. They might find things out using a CD-ROM and learn how to copy useful information from the CD-ROM to their work. They can add data to a database. They can use spreadsheets or database programs to prepare and examine graphs, and to search for patterns in data. They might use a branching database program to classify a set of creatures.
Children should use sensors - devices which measure temperature, light or sound in their investigations. They might develop a simple control system and perhaps also use sensors in their control project. They will learn to compare using IT with using other methods.

Assessing information technology

Historically, information technology skills have been sorted into several 'strands' or processes:

· Handling information - which you do when you use database and spreadsheet programs.

· Measuring and controlling - which you do when you use sensors and control technology.

· Modelling - which you can do when you use spreadsheet and modelling programs.

· Communicating with IT - which you do when you use word processors and graphics programs.

· The applications and effects of IT - which you can consider as you use information technology.

These strands embrace much of the information technology activity that takes place in school.

The tables on these pages show the sorts of things children might be doing and how these activities using IT become increasingly challenging as they progress through each of those strands. The aim has been to unpack some the coded language on the National Curriculum - rather than present an achieve-that-by-doing-this list.

Handling information

Progression in handling information with information technology	What the children do in science	IT level
Explore information held on IT systems.	Go to the computer. Use a CD-ROM and find a picture of a snail, see how it moves, hear/read about what they eat.	Level 1
Use IT to sort and classify information and to present their findings.	Find out how each child prefers their eggs cooked. Enter the results into a graph drawing program and display this as a graph or pictogram.	Level 2
Use IT to save data and access stored information, following straightforward lines of enquiry.	Look at a CD-ROM on animals and show all the animals that live in the jungle. Keep a record of what you found.	Level 3
Can add to, amend and interrogate stored information. They understand the need for care in framing questions when collecting, accessing and interrogating information. Interpret their findings, question plausibility and recognise that poor quality information yields unreliable results.	Use *BodyMapper* software to add your height, hair colour and other details to an existing class database. Check the details and correct mistakes. Sort the list of children into order of height and find answers to questions such as who is the tallest. Add a few pieces of incorrect data for the children to find.	Level 4
Select the information needed for different purposes, check its accuracy and organize and prepare it in a form suitable for processing using IT.	Do a survey of children in the class, starting with a list of questions that the survey will answer. Select the information you need to collect. Collect and organize the survey results into a class database. Check the data you entered and correct any errors. Process the information i.e. search it, sort it and draw graphs to answer your questions.	Level 5
Use complex lines of enquiry to test hypotheses.	Use a database on minibeasts to find all the creatures with six legs and two wings. Find out what they eat. Compare the foods of these creatures with those who have four wings.	Level 6

1

Assessing information technology

Measuring and controlling things

Progression in measuring and controlling things	What the children do in science	IT level
Recognise that everyday devices respond to signals and commands and they can make them respond in different ways.	Talk about how to use a video recorder.	Level 1
Control devices purposefully and describe the effects of their actions.	Technology: Use a floor robot.	Level 2
Understand how to control equipment to achieve specific outcomes by giving a series of instructions.	Technology: Understand how to control a robot and get it to go to the window and come back.	Level 3
Use IT to control events in a predetermined manner, to collect physical data and display it.	Technology: Get a floor robot to visit places on a model farm on the floor. Use sensors to record the temperature of their hands as they rub them together. Display and interpret the readings on the screen.	Level 4
Create sets of instructions to control events, and become sensitive to the need for precision in framing and sequencing instructions.	Technology: Get a floor robot to visit places on a picture of a farm on the floor. Be sensitive to the need to give precise instructions.	Level 5
Develop, trial and refine sets of instructions to control events, demonstrating an awareness of the notions of efficiency and economy in framing these instructions. Understand how IT devices can be used to monitor and measure external events, using sensors.	Technology: Control a robot, make it perform a set routine and look for more simple ways to do this. Use sensors to make measurements, for example, to measure their reaction time. Or use temperature sensors to compare the cooling of a cup of tea and a vacuum flask of tea.	Level 6

Modelling

Progression in using computer models and simulations	What the children do in science	IT level
Use IT-based models or simulations to investigate options as they explore aspects of real and imaginary situations.	Use a program like *Zoo Keeper:* the children have to feed and shelter animals in an appropriate way. *	Level 2
Use IT-based models or simulations to help them make decisions and be aware of the consequences of their choices.	Use a program such as *Badger Trails* to feed a badger and navigate one home past hazards such as roads.	Level 3
Use IT-based models or simulations to explore patterns and relationships, and make simple predictions about the consequences of their decision making.	Use the program *Botanical Gardens* to study the growth of seeds under different conditions. Use a spreadsheet program to study data on the planets. Look for patterns in the data. Suggest ideas such as 'the planets get hotter as they get closer to the sun'.	Level 4
Explore the effects of changing the variables in a computer model.	Experiment with a spreadsheet model of the use electricity in the home. Or use the program *At Home in Wattville* to find ways to save electricity at home.	Level 5
Use computer models of increasing complexity, vary the rules within them, and assess the validity of these models by comparing their behaviour with other data.	Experiment with a spreadsheet model of a person's daily use of energy.	Level 6

* See the Ideas section for details and programs for other topics.

1

Assessing information technology

Communicating with IT

Progression in communicating with information technology	What the children do in science	IT level
Use IT to assemble text and symbols to help them communicate ideas.	Prepare a captioned picture using a word processor. Arrange and label pictures in *My World* (TAG).	Level 1
Use IT to help them generate and communicate ideas in different forms, such as text, tables, pictures and sound. With some support, they retrieve and store work.	Prepare a poster using a word processor and add pictures to it. With help they can go back to it and finish it later.	Level 2
Use IT to generate, amend, organize and present ideas.	Prepare a poster using a word processor and add pictures to it. Come back to it and improve on it.	Level 3
Use IT to combine different forms of information, and show an awareness of their audience.	Use a word processor to prepare an investigation report for a school newsletter.	Level 4
Use IT to organize, refine and present information in different forms and styles for specific purposes and audiences.	Take an investigation report and re-work it to make an information leaflet.	Level 5
Develop and refine work using information from a range of sources, and demonstrating a clear sense of their audience and purpose in their presentation.	Make an advertisement for aluminium metal using words and graphics.	Level 6

Applications and effects of IT

Progression with the applications and effects of information technology	What the children do in science	IT level
Describe their use of IT, and its use in the outside world.	Discuss how scientists or others might use the IT tools that they use.	Level 3
Compare their use of IT with other methods.	Each time the children use a new IT tool, discuss its advantages and disadvantages. For example, discuss how a class database compares with a class register. Or compare the graphs the computer draws with the ones they draw by hand.	Level 4
Communicate their knowledge and experience of using IT and assess its use in their working practices.	Children explain how sensors help them to investigate science.	Level 5
Discuss the wider impact of IT on society.	Talk about the uses of sensors in everyday life, about interactive television and the information superhighway.	Level 6

1

Database programs

Today's scientists need **database programs** to handle their data. They may search through a database on disc, CD-ROM, or even on the Internet. They use their science skills to collect, organise and analyse data. They think carefully and look for patterns, they think critically and check data for errors. They will see how their findings fit other peoples'. Using a database in school parallels these processes.

Database programs allow you to store, sort and graph the results of a survey. If you had a database of children's personal data, you could sort the children into order of shoe size, or work out the average for the class. You could draw a bar chart to see how the shoe sizes vary across the class. Or draw a scattergraph to see if shoe sizes vary with the children's height. You might also search for all those with black hair and see if they have any eye colour in common. Using a database provides many opportunities to analyse data. It is a great tool for exploring science.

There are now many ready-made databases, usually on CD-ROM, that you can use. You will find titles on minibeasts, planets, mammals, birds and plants. They provide an amazing bank of data to look at in ways you could not do with the same in a book. These CD-ROM 'databases' have photographs, animation and they even talk making them useful with younger pupils.

Children can also learn to make databases. They can study themselves or survey opinion. Either way, when they make a database they have to be quite scientific in how they work. They have to define what they want to find out, collect the data, organise and analyse it. The pages that follow show how to do this.

IT tools

Section

2

Database glossary

Alphanumeric field - a type of field where you can store a mixture of numbers and letters.

Choice field - a type of field which gives you a list of items to choose from. A 'choice field' for eye colour could list blue, black, brown and green while, in a weather database, a choice field might offer dull, bright, cloudy and so on. Using this type of field can not only prevent errors and inconsistencies when you enter your data, it also encourages children to classify the objects in their database. When you use a database program in science, look for this feature.

Database - a collection of data about one topic. In school practice a database is a file of records. A commercial database can be a massive number of files about one topic.

Field length - tells the computer how much space an item of data takes up. The length of the field is measured in characters or key presses, i.e. the name red robin takes up 9 spaces, but you need extra space for longer names such as woodpecker.

Field types - different types of data need different field types. The most common field types are number and word types. Numbers often need units such as cm and kg.

Field - a *field* is the part of a file which stores a piece of information. A file might have fields storing 120cm, blue and 6.

Field names - often called headings or labels. For example, these are headings: height, eye colour and shoe size.

File - a collection of records. In practice it is what you save on the disc.

Chart - a feature to draw pie, bar and line graphs with the data. See the *Graphs glossary* on the next page.

Numeric field - a type of field where you can store numbers only. You need a numeric field to store heights and weights.

Pictogram - a very useful type of chart using symbols instead of bars. The symbols can be coloured blocks or pictures such as a stack of cars, aeroplanes or other symbol.

Records - a set of fields about one thing is called a record. The form you fill in on the screen about one thing or person is called a record.

Scattergraph - shows you if there is a pattern between two numeric fields such as between height and shoe-size. The scattergraph plots the fields as a series of dots and as you look along the dots, a line through them suggests a pattern. These are very useful but children rarely understand them. One work-around is to sort the data on say height, plot a bar chart of shoe-size and then see if the bars show a pattern.

Search - lets you select out certain records - e.g. search for all the people with brown eyes. You can do 'complex' searches where you search for all the people with brown eyes and black hair - so you can use a search to hunt for a pattern.

Spreadsheet - another type of program which can handle data. These programs share many features in common with database programs. If your set of data is quite small, say, just 10 records and you just want to draw graphs, a spreadsheet may be a better choice.

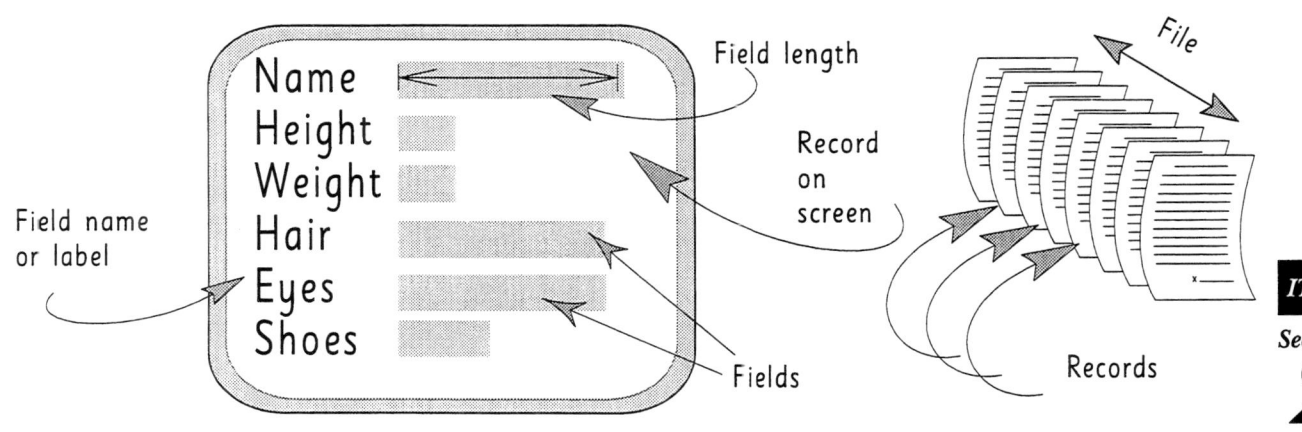

Graphs glossary

One of our roles as teachers is to encourage children to communicate effectively using graphs. Computers draw them with great ease - in fact, when you use databases and spreadsheets you can produce an astounding range of graphs to analyse your surveys.

Here then are some working descriptions of the most popular and useful kinds of graph you will meet on the computer.

Histograms and count graphs

These give an idea of the spread of your results. For the chart here, the insect lengths were divided into five ranges and counted. The graph shows the number of insects which have similar lengths. Histograms, unlike bar charts, show which ranges are the most significant and whether the results are well spread. Some programs let you make pictograms - showing pictures instead of bars. These are essential.

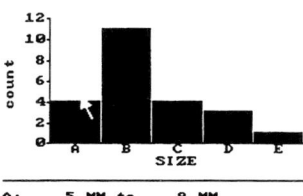

Pie charts

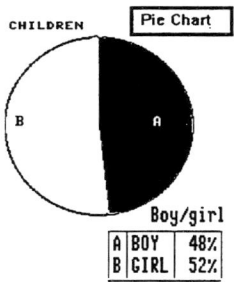

One of the easiest charts for comparing parts with a total. For example, you can draw a pie chart to see what proportion of a class are girls. When you use a *database* a pie chart might show you, for example, the spread of the shoe sizes in the class. (For obscure reasons, the same pie chart in a spreadsheet may not).

Bar or column chart

The bar chart is a generic title. There are stacked bar charts, histograms and more. On a computer, a bar chart shows the spread of the results. For example, a bar chart of children's heights shows each child with a bar representing their height. A histogram of the same data would divide the class into ranges and count the number falling in each range.

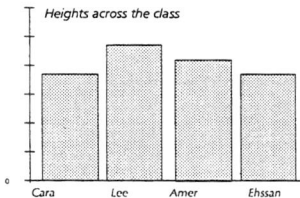

Scattergraphs or X-Y graphs

A useful graph for science, but hard to understand. They help to find a pattern between two sets of numbers or variables - for example, to find out if larger animals have larger wingspans. Usually *(see below)* you see a pattern of dots - rather than a line of best fit.

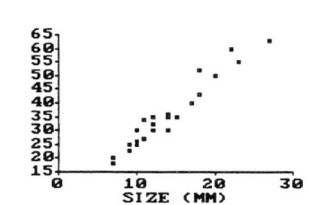

Venn diagrams

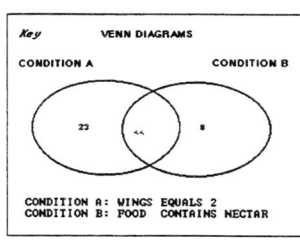

Useful for seeing if there is a connection between different features, for example, do minibeasts with two wings feed on nectar? The circles show how many creatures have each feature, while the overlap shows how many have both features.

Line graphs

Computers, like children, think that line graphs are just bar graphs drawn with a line instead of bars. For example, you can use a computer line graph to show how a plant grows over time. (However, you must make sure that your readings were taken at equal intervals - be that days or weeks). These line graphs have similar uses to bar graphs but they show gradual changes better. If, in fact, you really want a graph where one set of numbers is plotted against another, ask for a scattergraph instead.

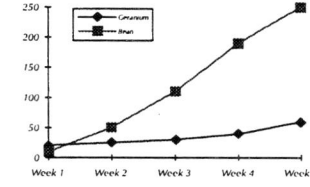

1. Making a database about your class

A database project positively needs planning. This page is a teacher's plan for a class database project. The following pages show the steps in more detail.

Starting from the basics

If the children have no experience of databases try the following as a preamble. Make a card-index database about the class and sort the cards in order of height. Pick out those with black hair and arrange them as a bar chart on the desk. Or you might arrange the children as a bar chart in the hall (cf. diagram above).

Look at a database of children's data.

Sort, search and graph a ready-made database. See the pages that follow on *Using graphs* which exemplify various ways to find things out with a computer.

Add your entry to the database.

Children can add their personal data to an existing database. They might then draw a bar chart, say of their heights and see where they appear. Following this dry-run they can set about preparing a database for real.

Decide what you want to find out.

You might want to know: who is the tallest in the class? Who is the oldest? Does arm reach have anything to do with height? Which eye colour is the most common? What are our favourite foods? Limit the number of questions: use 3 or 4 questions with younger groups, use six or seven questions with older groups. See the sheet on *Doing a survey* for a suggested approach.

Decide on the information you need to collect.

For example you might collect details of height, birth date, shoe size, arm reach, eye colour, hair colour and favourite food. You will need to be sensitive to children being permanently labelled 'shortest' or whatever. Measuring fingers and thumbs is a work around.

Decide on how you will collect the information.

List all of the items of data you need to collect on a questionnaire. Also list the units to use, for example, height in cm, gender as B or G, birthdate as YYMMDD, eye colour - choice of blue, black, brown or green, favourite food as choice of beans (not baked beans), chips (not fries). Print off the questionnaires and collect the data.

Check the information for mistakes.

Check the completed sheets for errors and inconsistency.

Create the heading (or field) names.

Some software will insist that you shorten long headings and sacrifice clarity: for example, 'hair colour' might have to be shortened to 'hair'. See the two sheets that follow called *About computer databases* and *Make a database for a survey*.

Enter the data.

The children can enter their information. They should save their work regularly.

Check the information in the computer.

Print out the information and check it.

Use the database to answer your questions

Look at the questions you started with. Use the database program to sort, graph and average to answer them. See the pages on *Using graphs* for examples.

Evaluate the work

The children may find this difficult. See the table in Section 1 on *Assessment - applications and effects of IT* for some of the points you might raise.

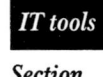

IT tools

Section

2

2. Doing a survey

What this is about

This page is about starting a survey to find out how much the children vary. For example, you might want to find out:

What is the most common hair colour?

What is the most common shoe size?

Who is the tallest?

Who is the oldest?

What is the average height?

How many children are taller than average?

Are younger people shorter?

What to do

Think of some questions you want to answer in your survey.

I want to answer these questions:

You now need to collect some information. What information do you need to collect?

I need to collect information about
Height

Use a word processor to make a questionnaire for your survey.

Test your questionnaire out on a friend and change your questions if they are not clear.

What this is about

This tells you how database programs organise information.

Organising information

We wanted to find out how much children vary so we collected some information from them.

We put our information under different headings. There was a heading for the name, a heading for how tall the people were, a heading for their shoe size, their hair colour, their eye colour and birthdate. The headings are called *field names*.

We entered the information about each child, in the spaces next to the headings. These spaces are called *fields*.

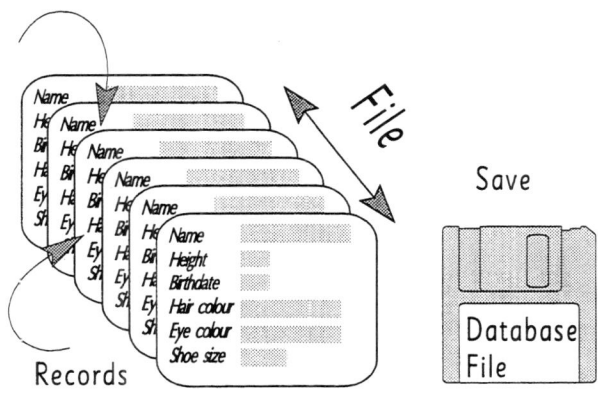

Database words: records and file

All the information about one child is called *a record*. We saved the records on a disk. All the records together make what computers call *a file*. (See figure)

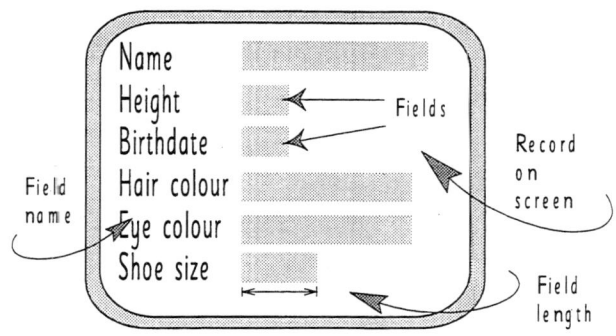

Database words: fields, field names and field lengths.

Which type of field?

The *fields* store information. This might be words, numbers, dates or choices.

The name field is *alphanumeric* - meaning that it can contains words, letters or numbers. The **name** 'Jo' is alphanumeric.

The height field is *numeric* - it contains numbers only. A **height** of '110' is numeric.

The **birth date** field is a *date* field. '6/6/88' is a date.

Hair colour is a *choice* field - when you enter your information, you choose from brown, black, blonde or red.

Some information takes up more space than others. We call this space the *field length*. For example, the field for **hair colour,** needs 6 letter spaces to store the colour 'blonde'.

Why do all this?

Once you have the information in the computer, you can sort it into order. You might sort the children into order of their height.

You can draw a pie chart. A pie chart can show you the hair colour in the class. A bar chart can show you the heights in the class. A scattergraph can show you if taller people have bigger feet.

You can search the information to find all those with black hair. You can go on to find if there is a pattern between those with black hair and those with brown eyes.

IT tools

Section

2

What this is about

Here you can make a database using the ideas on the previous page.

What you did

You have just done a survey of the people in your group. You now want to make a database to store the information you have collected.

For example, you collected the following data. The table shows you six *fields* belonging to one *record* in our database.

Data collected	For example
Name	Jo Smiff
Date of birth	12/3/85
Height	110 cm
Hair colours	Black
Shoe size	6 cm
Shoulder size	60 cm

What to do

Start to make your database by filling in the diagram below:

Write in the field names or headings you will use

Write in one record from your survey.

Write in the types of field you will use: some will be numeric, some alphanumeric and some will be choice fields.

Mark the field length - how many character spaces you need.

Write the field names here | Fill in one record here | Write the field types here | Mark the field lengths here

Eye colour | Brown | Choice | 6

5. Using graphs

What this is about

This page shows how you can use a computer to look at your data. You will need to choose the best type of chart to draw.

Choose the best chart

This information is about a class of children. Across the top are the field names or headings.

Name	Colour of Eyes	Colour of Hair	Height cm	Weight kg	Shoe Size	Boy/ Girl
Sertac	Brown	Black	129	29	3	Boy
Geoffrey	Blue	Brown	131	30	3	Boy
Ehssan	Brown	Black	131	32	3	Boy
Yit Kwon	Brown	Brown	138	32	4	Boy
Sonia	Blue	Brown	130	33	3	Girl
Tony	Hazel	Blond	133	34	2	Boy
Cara	Blue	Blond	137	37	5	Girl
Alistair	Brown	Black	132	37	4	Boy
Sam. A	Brown	Black	143	38	5	Boy
Sam. M	Brown	Black	137	39	5	Boy
Nahum	Brown	Black	142	40	5	Boy
Mustafa	Brown	Black	137	41	3	Boy
Paula	Brown	Brown	144	42	5	Girl
Andy	Brown	Black	143	42	5	Boy
Lee	Blue	Blond	142	43	4	Boy
Derek	Brown	Brown	145	43	4	Boy
Yucel	Blue	Brown	147	44	5	Boy
Amer	Brown	Black	144	47	5	Boy
Victor	Brown	Black	151	51	7	Boy

One way of using the computer to find things out is to draw graphs. For example, we wanted to find out about the mixture of boys and girls - so we drew a pie chart using the Boy/Girl field:

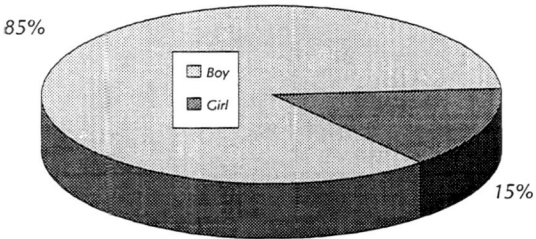

85%

| Boy
| Girl

15%

Boys and girls in our class

What does this chart tell you?

We wanted to find out about the class' shoe sizes so we drew a pie chart of the shoe size:

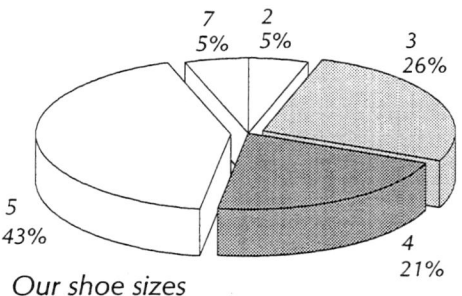

7 5% 2 5% 3 26%

5 43%

4 21%

Our shoe sizes

What are the two most common shoe sizes?

We also drew a bar chart of the Shoe size:

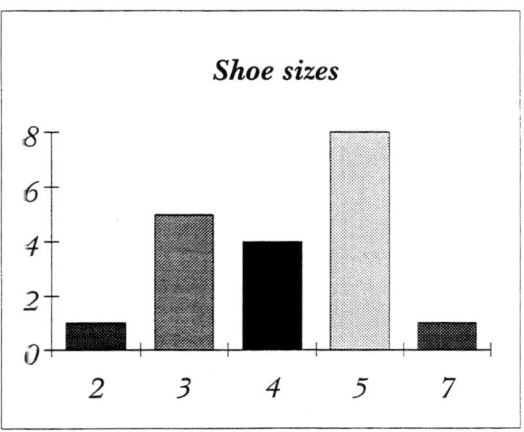

Shoe sizes

8
6
4
2
0

2   3   4   5   7

Questions

Compare the **bar chart** with the **pie chart** above. Which best shows the shoe sizes across the class?

How could you find the most common hair colours in the class?

What this is about

This page shows how you can use a computer to look at your data. You sort a list, work out an average and draw a chart.

Showing how we vary

We collected some information about children: their heights, weights and shoe sizes. We worked out the average weight of a child and then set about finding how everyone's weights varied by drawing a bar chart:

However, this was not very useful. We cannot easily see how many are above or below the average weight. We therefore decided to sort the class in order of weight and draw the bar chart again:

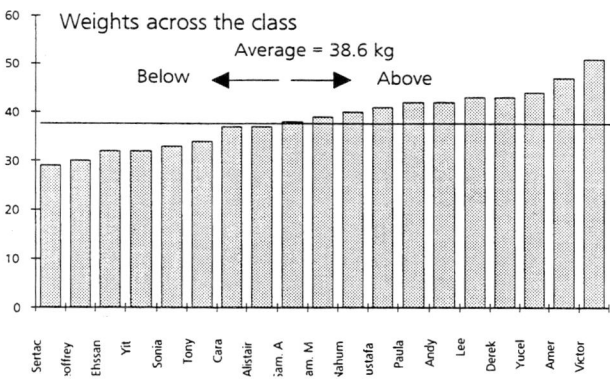

How many children are above the average weight?

Looking for patterns

You can look for patterns by drawing a **scattergraph**. We wondered if there was a pattern between height and weight so we made a scattergraph of height against weight:

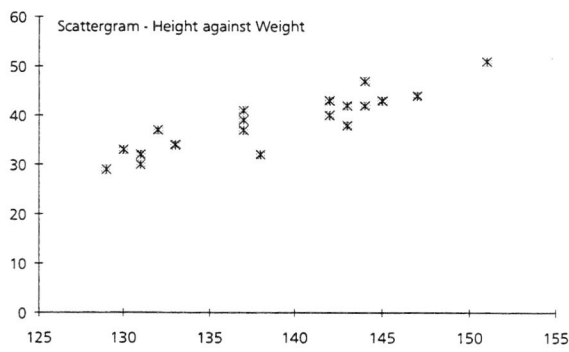

If you can see a trend in the points you may have found a pattern. What does the chart above tell you?

Showing the most common results

We wanted to find the most common weights in the class so we drew a **histogram**. This is a type of bar chart where all the data is arranged in groups.

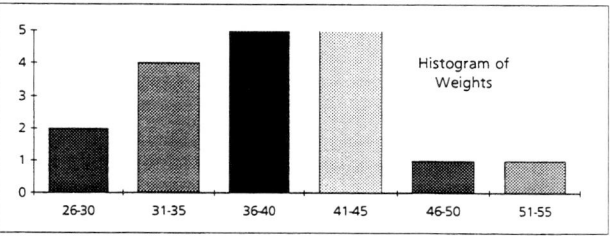

What are the most common weight groups in the class?

Using your own database

Use your database to find answers to the following:

How many children are above the average height? *(Find the average and sort the list. Draw a bar chart)*

Do taller children wear bigger shoes? *(Draw a scattergraph of shoe size against height).*

What are the most common heights in the class? *(Draw a histogram of the children's heights).*

IT tools

Section
2

What this is about

In this activity you hunt for minibeasts hidden in a computer database or CD-ROM

You have just found the following creatures - use a computer database to identify them.

What to do

Get your computer database on minibeasts on the screen. Use the clues and search the database to find and identify the creatures below.

What is this?

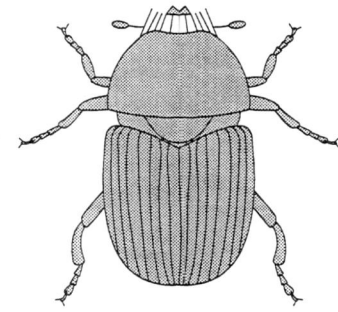

We saw this creature under a log. It has a red body.

How many legs does it have?

Can it fly?

We found this creature on the garden compost heap.

What is it?

What does it eat?

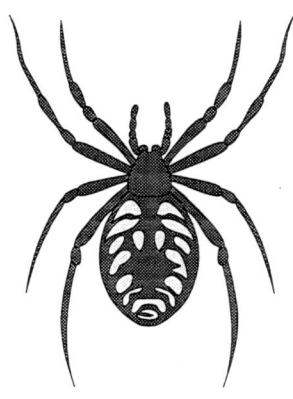

We found this minibeast too.

What is it?

What colour is it?

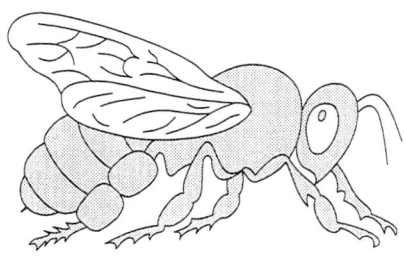

We saw this in some flowers.

Where else might you find it?

What does it eat?

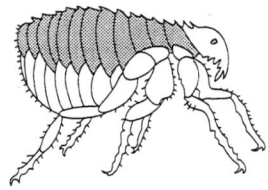

This creature moves fast.

What colour is it?

How does it move?

Note:

This is the sort of introductory activity you can build around a database or CD-ROM on minibeasts or animals. This particular example used the Key Minibeasts database from Anglia TV. This is good but is overshadowed by modern CD-ROM databases such as Anglia's **Garden Wildlife**. Look in the Ideas section for details.

IT tools

Section

2

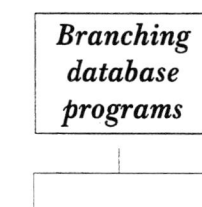

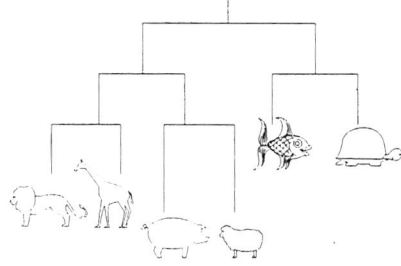

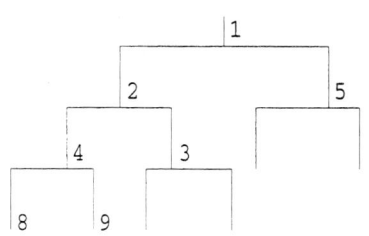

Branching database programs

A **branching database** is a special kind of database. We use it to classify things and build up a key. It helps us sort out sets of animals, plants and almost anything else. Like ordinary database programs, the branching database stores data. Unlike them, the data is stored as a branching key as in the example here,

1. Does it live in water?
   If yes go to 5   If no go to 2

2. Does it live in the jungle?
   If yes go to 4   If no go to 3

3. ...

4. Does it have a long neck?
   If yes go to 9   If no go to 8

5. ...

8. Is it a lion?

9. Is it a giraffe?

10. ...

The value of using a branching database comes from getting the children to build up a key for themselves. With many activities in this book we use technology because it helps us produce some end-product or that the product is better or even that it saves time. However, we use a branching database because it provides a surprisingly strong focus for getting children to think about the things they classify. They will use and develop a variety of science skills - they observe, question, discuss and classify. For this reason branching database activities can be good science and even a cornerstone of the best.

Projects with a branching database can be improved with a little structuring. The next page shows the general plan, while the one following sets this out more formally.

1. Make a branching database on animals

How you might run a branching database activity is the subject of the following two pages.

Play '20 questions' to identify some animals.

The 20 Questions game gets the children to practise the idea of asking questions which have a yes or no answer. A set of animal cards, made  from photographs from magazines and stuck onto card are a good stimulus. You can spell their names and add key features on the back of each card. The children play the '20 Questions' game with the 'leader' picking up one card at a time.

Introduce the computer program.

Use a ready-made branching database. Pick up an animal card and work through the program - these are quite structured programs so there are no real operational points to consider. Get the computer to identify the animal. Let the children get the hang of this.

Leave the computer.

Now get the children to sort all the animal cards into sets. Get them to record the reasons for putting things into sets like 'Lives in water' and 'Doesn't live in water'. They can label them with a *Post-it* note or similar.

Arrange the animal cards to make a key.

If you wish, use ribbon or paper strips to link the sets together, like a key, as in the diagram above.

Return to the computer.

Start a new database using just two animals, one from two different sets. Do this yourself and then get the group to think of a question to distinguish one animal from the other. The key works just a bit better when you start off with more general questions such as, 'Does it live in water' rather than 'Does it meow'? With younger groups you can economise on the words used - and enter questions like 'Meow?' or 'Live in water?'

Build up the database.

The children now pick up one card at a time and work through the program. As they do so the database will grow. The *Post-it* labels with the questions on can be to hand as prompts. The children should work in groups of two or three. In larger groups things can get boring quite quickly. A group of three can take turns to pick an animal, think of a question and use the keyboard. Children should save their work frequently. If they make a mistake it's often easier to get the last good copy back off the disc rather than try to puzzle out what has gone wrong.

Get the others to test the key.

Children can try out the key and suggest ways to improve the questions. You can use the finished database both as a handy key and to introduce the activity next time around.

IT tools

Section

2

2. Sorting out musical instruments

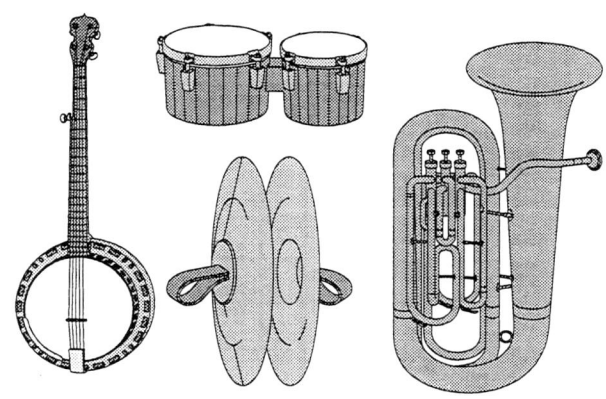

What this is about

The children use a branching database program to build an identification key for musical instruments. The children will need to observe carefully, sort things out, work methodically and test their ideas. This page sets out how you might run this activity - adding some ideas which focus on the science of music rather than other aspects.

Good starting point

You can start by talking about musical instruments and how we can sort them out into families. You might focus on how they work (moving strings, moving air) rather than where they come from.

You may have a CD-ROM of musical instruments to 'bring' less common instruments into the classroom.

What to do

Play the game *Twenty questions*. In this game, one member of the group plays the 'thinker'. The others have to guess the musical instrument they are thinking of.

What to say to the 'thinker'

You have to think of a musical instrument. Choose one you know something about. You might choose from a flute, a violin, a guitar or a drum. The others have to guess what it is by asking questions. You can only answer their questions with a 'yes' or a 'no'.

What to say to the others:

You have to guess the musical instrument by asking the 'thinker' questions. Your questions will only get a yes or no answer. To make the game more scientific, you have to ask questions about how the instrument works, what it is made from or what makes the sound. For example:

You may ask: "does it have strings" but not "does it begin with 'p' "

You may ask: "is it made of wood?" but not "is it brown?"

You may ask "do you play it by blowing ... ?" but not "do you play it on the floor?"

Playing the computer sorting game

Get the *Sorting game*** program running.

Use the old game called *Music* on the disc and start the game.

Think of an organ and answer yes or no to the questions.

If the computer guesses the organ correctly, think of another and play the game again.

If the computer gives up and asks you what it is, tell it. Then, very carefully, follow the instructions on the screen.

Save your work on the disc from time to time. Do not save any mistakes on the disc.

Continue until your time is up.

Note

The children will appreciate having a book of musical instruments. As the instructions show, it is quite important not to enter the wrong questions and answers. To get off to a healthy start, 'prime' the computer with two instruments before the children begin. Simply, get the program running and start a new game called *Music*. You might then enter two instruments, the flute and the piano and the question "does it have strings?"

*These are also known as branching database, tree database, sorting game, dichotomous key or binary key programs. See the Reference section for titles.

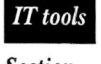

Section

2

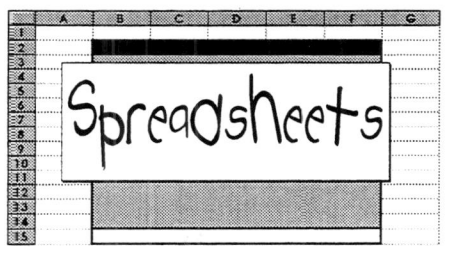

Spreadsheets, graphs and calculations

A **spreadsheet** is very much a multipurpose program. You can use one as a ready-made results table and quickly produce a graph from it. You can also use one as a data handling program to sort your results and again produce graphs from it.

These are important things to learn to do - though you don't have to use a spreadsheet for them. There are special **graph drawing programs** and pictogram making programs that do graphs more easily - though you might feel that your spreadsheet program is easy enough. But at some point, towards the top of the primary school, it is worth moving on to a spreadsheet. At this level, you can use an interesting feature of a spreadsheet - its ability to do calculations and make 'mathematical models'.

	A	B	C
1	Body	Gravity	Your weight
2	Earth	1.0	40
3	Moon	0.2	6
4	Mercury	0.4	15
5	Mars	0.4	15
6	Venus	0.9	34
7	Uranus	1.0	40
8	Saturn	1.1	44
9	Neptune	1.5	60
10	Jupiter	2.6	104
11			
12	MAXIMUM	2.6	104
13	MINIMUM	0.2	6.4

A mathematical model allows you try something out - perhaps without actually doing it. If you had, for example, some information about the gravity on the planets and the moon, you could get the spreadsheet to work out how much you would weigh on each of these. First, you would enter the gravity information and then write a 'formula' to do the maths. There is nothing really special about a formula - it's merely algebra. For example, in the spreadsheet here, you only need to enter your real weight in cell C2 to see what you would weigh on the moon in cell C3. Cell C3 calculates your weight on the moon and contains the algebra or formula C2 x B3. This spreadsheet is a mathematical model - it is the alternative to actually going to the moon to weigh yourself.

Spreadsheets have an astonishing range of functions that can help with maths or modelling. They can total or average columns, look for maximum or minimum values and turn any mathematical trick.

The following pages illustrate how you can use a spreadsheet - progressing from easy graph drawing to more difficult 'models'. The ideas show how versatile these programs are in organising, recording and analysing your results - all of which are key features of exploring science.

IT tools

Section

2

Spreadsheet glossary

Bar chart - a graph plotted with a bar for every result.

Cell reference - every cell has a reference code you can use to refer to it. The spreadsheet columns are labelled from A to Z while the rows are labelled from 1 to 100. A columns of cells would be A1, A2, A3 ...

Cells - the boxes on the screen into which you type your results.

Copy - a feature to copy something you've typed, saving you having to type it again.

Data - the numbers and words that you've collected together.

Database program - like a spreadsheet this a program for handling data. When you have lots of data it's better to use a database program. But use a spreadsheet if your results fit into a table and if your data is mostly numbers. Spreadsheets are good if you want to do calculations or if you want to see all your results in one glance.

Formula - you make a formula when you need to do some maths, such as multiply two numbers together. Cell references are used in building spreadsheet formulae - for example, the following formula works out a percentage: *=100 * B2/B3*

Function - a formula which is built into the spreadsheet. It can work out the total or average of a column.

Labels - the headings for the spreadsheet table.

Line graph - like a bar chart but a line is drawn where the bar tops would be.

Move - a feature which moves something you've typed to a new place on the spreadsheet. It saves you having to type it again.

Name - you can highlight a cell and give it a memorable name. You might name one cell 'distance' and another cell 'time'. You could then type in a formula that made more sense, i.e. to calculate a speed, you would type =distance/time instead of say, C3/B4.

Operator - meaning arithmetic operators such as multiply, divide, add and subtract or * / + - .

Pie Chart - a chart which can show the relative numbers of, say girls and boys in the class. The result is shown as percentages.

Range - is a set of cells. In *C3:C8*, the range is the set of cells stretching from cell C3 to C8.

Scattergraph - an x-y graph you can use to find patterns in your results.

Sort - a feature which sorts a column into order. You mark or select the column you want to sort. You will be asked if you want to sort it into ascending or descending order. Words are sorted into alphabetical order. Note that the computer 'alphabet' begins with numbers so that in an address: *7 Heathview* comes before *Heathview*. Similarly when you sort numbers into alphabetical order, the result is that 11 comes before 7.

Values - these are the numbers and words that you've collected and entered on a spreadsheet.

Spreadsheet jargon

Cell Reference Each cell has a **cell reference**. This is A1

Labels Headings for the table.

Cell Each box in the table is called a **cell**.

	A	B	C
1			
2		Gravity %	Your weight
3	Earth	100	40
4	Moon	20	6
5	Mercury	40	15
6	Mars	40	15
7	Venus	90	34
8	Uranus	100	40
9			
10	MAXIMUM	100	40
11	MINIMUM	20	6

Values The data you've collected and typed in.

Formula This cell does some maths using a **formula**.. Your weight gets worked out with the formula: B5*C3

Function a built-in formula. This cell will find the maximum weight. This function looks like: MAX(C3:C8) You can also do averages.

IT tools

Section

2

 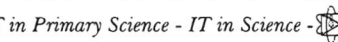

Teaching and spreadsheets

Teaching progression

The spreadsheet is probably the most versatile data handling tool we have. We can take the many skills involved in using one and put them into a 'progression ladder' as shown below. The top few rungs on the ladder can be achieved by using graph drawing programs, and younger children will gain access to some difficult ideas by using them. You'll need a spreadsheet to create models and do calculations. You can model how much electricity we use at home, or how much energy we use doing different activities. And if you set these up for the children, they need only add their numbers to have the difficult maths done for them.

In fact, the skills at the bottom of the table are very hard to develop with a spreadsheet. It might even be better not to use a spreadsheet at all here. Perhaps more accessible tools - science programs could be used instead. There is a lot of ready-made and very good modelling software in the shops. There is a program that uses a picture of the home, complete with appliances, to show how much electricity we use. Another, lets you enter the food you eat and draws graphs to tell you if you are eating the right things. There is little doubt that these are better and easier to use, but this advantage has to be balanced against the value of teaching children about spreadsheets.

Nevertheless, the children will benefit from plenty of exposure to spreadsheets. They remain valuable for so many recording tasks.

Progression in data handling and modelling skills	
Using a graphing program or spreadsheet as a recording table.	IT Level 2
Using a graphing program or spreadsheet as a recording table. Sorting and graphing	IT Level 3
Saving and retrieving work on disc.	IT Level 3
Interpreting graphs and questioning their plausibility.	IT Level 4
Using a spreadsheet with built-in calculations as a model.	IT Level 4
Graphing one variable against another in a scattergraph and finding patterns.	IT Level 4
Changing formulae in a spreadsheet model to see how this affects the results.	IT Level 5 / 6

How do you like your eggs?

What this is about

The children do a survey on their favourite way of cooking eggs. They use a graph drawing or pictogram drawing program. The children use IT here to 'sort information and present their findings'. They learn too about collecting and recording results.

Starting points

Discuss the ways we cook eggs and the foods that have eggs in them.

How could they record how everyone likes their eggs cooked?

What to do

Make a recording table using your graph or pictogram drawing program. One group can collect the results or each child can, in turn, add their entries to the table.

Get the program to produce a graph. For example, this is a regular bar graph - however, your graph drawing program may be capable of doing graphs like those opposite.

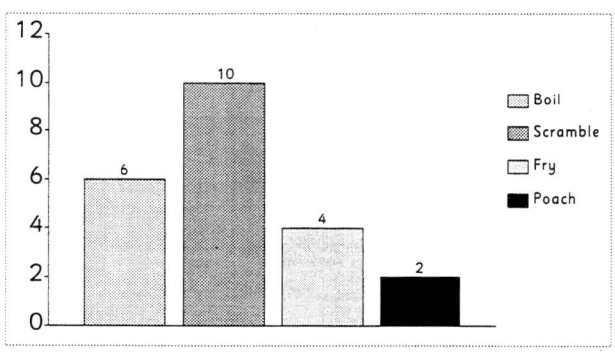

Questions to ask

What does the graph show? Which graph is best?

Which is the most popular cooked egg?

Extra

Get everyone to score each way of cooking eggs on a scale of one to five. Use a spreadsheet to add up your class' scores and put these on a graph.

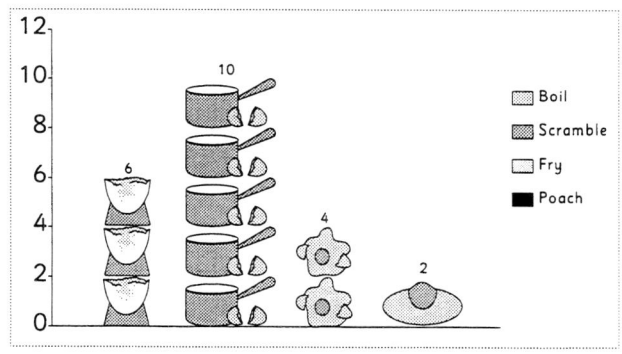

IT tools

Section
2

Where do plants grow best?

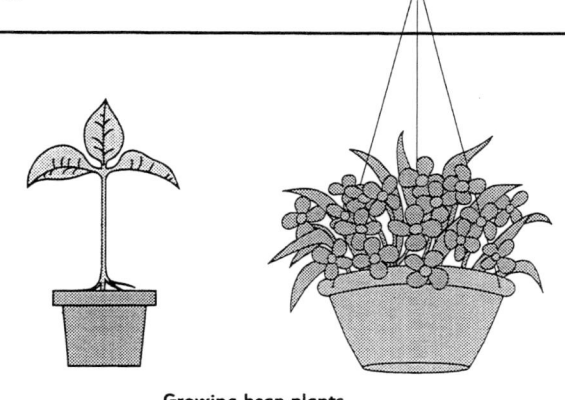

What this is about

The children investigate plants growing under different conditions, for example, in and out of the light. They measure them daily and use a spreadsheet to record their results. They draw a graph. The children use IT here to 'sort information and present their findings'. They learn too about the conditions for plant growth and how fast they grow.

If you have a pictogram drawing program, the children may be able to make a more interesting graph as shown below.

Starting points

Discuss the best and worst places to grow plants. How can you test your ideas?

Discuss how you could measure how much a plant has grown.

What to do

Set up pots with bean seeds. Place these in the light, the dark, the fridge and so on.

Measure how long the stems are every three days. Record your results in a pictogram program or spreadsheet. If you wish, produce a graph each time you add a new set of results.

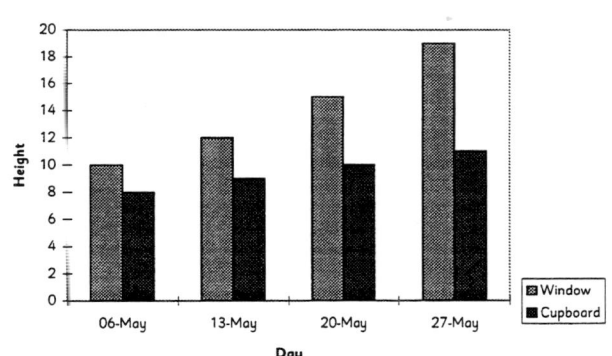

Growing bean plants

Questions to ask

What does the graph tell you about places to grow things?

Which things make a lot of difference? Which do not?

Where in the school grounds would you put your favourite plant?

Extra

Can a plant have too little / too much water?

Growing plants		
	cm	cm
	Window	**Cupboard**
06-May	10	8
13-May	12	9
20-May	15	10
27-May	19	11

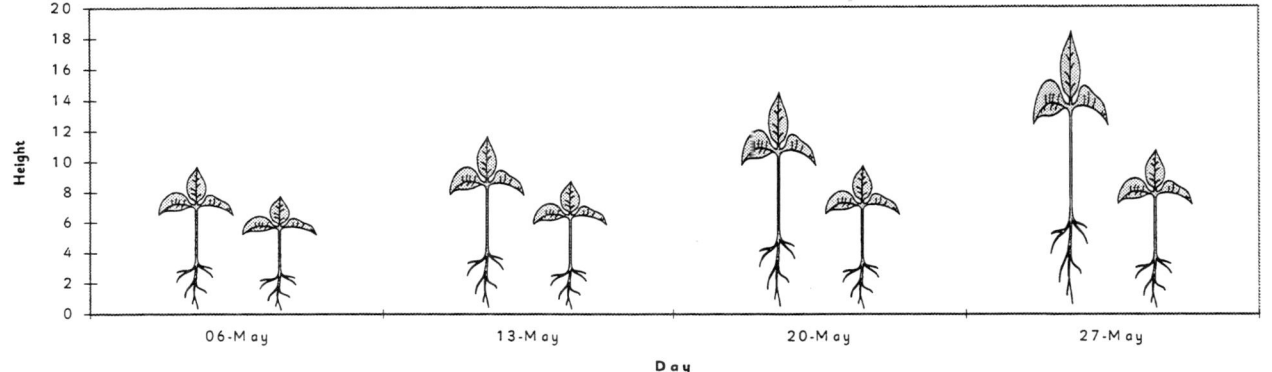

IT tools

Section

2

Which bridge is stronger?

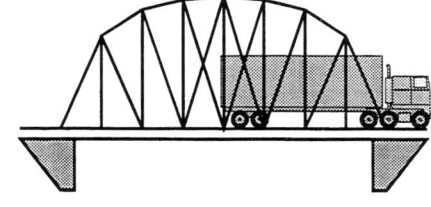

What this is about

This activity uses a spreadsheet to record some results. The children test different bridges and use their results to draw a graph. The children use IT here to 'sort information and present their findings'. They learn too about structures and balanced forces.

As shown below, you can extend that idea and use the graph to predict whether a bridge will get stronger if you use more paper to make it. Here they would be using IT to 'explore a real situation'.

Starting points

Discuss the huge loads that bridges carry. Why did London bridge fall down? Which bridge design might be best?

How could we make our bridges stronger? If we used more material the bridge would be stronger, but can we say how strong a bridge will be without actually making it?

You will need

A spreadsheet, tape, scissors, weights, 'piers' and soft card.

What to do

Use a piece of card to build a bridge to span a 15 cm gap. Here are some bridge design ideas:

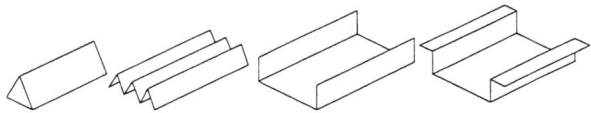

Test the bridge with weights to see how much it can take.

Record your results in a spreadsheet as shown.

Bridge design	
Bridge	How many weights it took
Cylinder	2
Square	4
Hat shape	3
Triangle	3

Questions to ask

Draw a bar graph. Which bridge design seems best? Is it a bit better, or a lot better than the others?

Extra

To extend the work you could make the same bridge using two, three, four and five pieces of card. Make these bridges and test them with weights.

How many sheets to make a strong bridge?		
Sheets of pape	No of weights taken	
1		
2		
3		
4		
5		
6	Do not make	
7	Do not make	

If you use more material, does the bridge get stronger? Highlight your results and draw a bar chart. Yours might look like this:

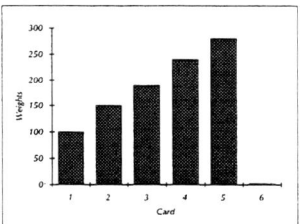

How many weights would a bridge with six pieces of card take? Draw a line through the tops of your bars in the chart. Try to read the answers from the graph. For example,

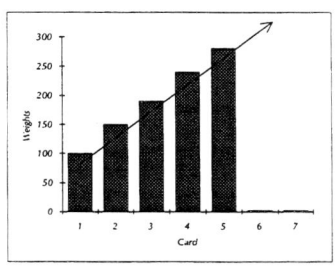

Write a letter to a Martian with some advice about building bridges.

How far does it go?

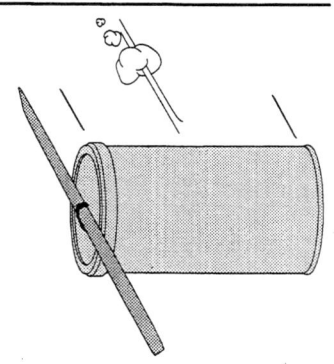

What this is about

When you wind up a cotton-reel roller you store energy in the elastic band. When you let go this energy is released and the roller moves forward. In this activity the children investigate cotton reel rollers. They use a spreadsheet to record their results and draw a graph. The spreadsheet also calculates an average - you could do this for them. The children use IT here to 'sort information and present their findings'. They learn too about 'elastic bands exerting forces'.

Starting points

How far would a cotton-reel roller travel on a level surface? Can the children make one go further? Does winding the elastic band more make a lot of difference?

Do you think that if you turned the band twice as far, the roller will go twice as far? Is there a pattern between the times you turn the band and how far it travels?

You will need

A spreadsheet, elastic bands, cotton reels, orange sticks.

What to do

Make a cotton reel roller. Wind up the roller different numbers of turns and measure how far it travels. Do this three times for each number of turns.

Make a spreadsheet and enter your results as shown below. The spreadsheet will calculate the average of three 'goes' with the roller.

You can plot a scattergraph of your results. Or you can use a bar graph instead - but make sure the 'number of turns' increases as you go down the spreadsheet.

	A	B	C	D	E
1	Cotton reel rollers				
2	Number of turns	Distance 1	Distance 2	Distance 3	Average distance
3		cm	cm	cm	cm
4	10	3	2	1	xx
5	20				xx
6	30				xx
7	40				xx
8	50				xx
9	60				xx
10					
11	**How to plot a graph**				
12	1. Highlight cells A4 to A9. 2. Hold down the CTRL key.				
13	3. Highlight cells E4 to E9				
14	4. Get the program to plot a bar or scattergraph.				

Questions to ask

Does turning the band more change how far it travels? Does it make a lot of difference?

Write about what you did for next year's class.

Extra

Would other elastic band powered toys show the same pattern?

	A	B	C	D	E	F	G	H	I
1	Cotton reel rollers								
2	Number of turns	Distance 1	Distance 2	Distance 3	Average distance				
3		cm	cm	cm	cm				
4	10	3	2	1	2				
5	20								
6	30								
7	40								
8	50								
9	60								
10									
11									
12									
13									
14									

How to set up your spreadsheet
1. Enter the headings in rows 1, 2 and 3.
2. Enter the number of turns of the elastic band in column A.
3. Measure how far the roller goes and record your reading in column B.
4. Do this for different numbers of turns.
5. Repeat this twice more. Enter your readings in column C and D.
6. Move to cell E4 and enter the formula =AVERAGE (B4:D4). This works out the average of your three results.
7. Copy cell E4. Paste it into cells E5 to E9.

IT tools

Section

2

What would you weigh on the moon?

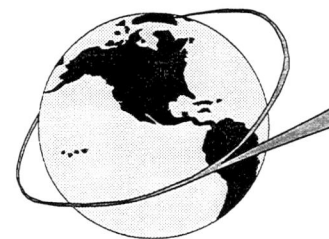

What this is about

This activity uses a spreadsheet to do a calculation and draw a graph. It shows you how to make a relatively easy spreadsheet 'model' - the IT skills required here are minimal - the interpretation of the graph is a bit harder. In curriculum speak: the children use this model to 'explore a real situation'.

The activity highlights that there is a different gravity pull on different planets. The children can look at the graph and say which planets have a lot or little gravity - in other words they draw a conclusion from their results.

Starting points

Ask the children what would happen if they tried to use bathroom scales in space. Would they weigh anything?

Watch some film of astronauts on the moon. Could they use scales on the moon? Would they weigh more, or less on the moon?

Look at a model of the solar system. Explain that the spreadsheet can work out how much they weigh in different places.

What to do

Start a new spreadsheet and follow the instructions in the diagram below.

Get each child to enter their weight in the box in the spreadsheet. They can then draw a graph.

Questions to ask

What do you weigh on earth?

What would you weigh on the moon?

On which planet or moon would you weigh the most?

Sort them into: those where you weigh a lot, and those where you weigh a little.

* We can't just use the word planet here because the moon is not a planet.

Extra

Use a spreadsheet to help you work out how to build a scale model of the solar system. The program should help you scale the distances of the planets from the sun. See the Ideas section.

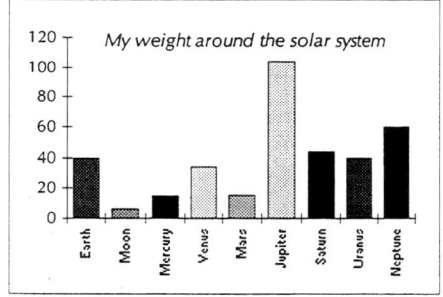

My weight around the solar system

How to draw a graph with your spreadsheet
1. Highlight cells A3 to A11
2. Hold down CTRL other special key.
3. Highlight cells C3 to C11
4. Get the program to draw a bar graph.

	A	B	C	D
1	How much would you weigh on ...?			
2	Body	Gravity	Your weight	
3	Earth	1	40	
4	Moon	0.16	6	
5	Mercury	0.37	15	
6	Venus	0.86	34	
7	Mars	0.38	15	
8	Jupiter	2.6	104	
9	Saturn	1.1	44	
10	Uranus	1	40	
11	Neptune	1.5	60	

How to set up your spreadsheet
1. Copy rows 1 and 2 as shown here.
2. Copy columns A and B as shown here.
3. Move to cell C3 and enter your weight.
4. Move to cell C4 and enter the formula =C3*B4
This works out your weight on the moon.
5. Copy cell C4.
Paste it into cells C5 to C11

How can we save electricity?

What this is about

This shows you how to make a spreadsheet 'model' of electricity use at home. It shows that different appliances use different amounts of electricity and that if you want to save money, cutting down some things is better than others. To quote the curriculum documents, the children use this 'IT-based model to help them make decisions'. If the children could create and use a spreadsheet like this you would say that they could 'design a computer model'.

Starting points

List all the things that use electricity at home. Which of these do you think, use the most electricity?

Get an electric kettle and a light bulb and look for the power ratings. Discuss which uses the most electricity and which you use the longest. The computer will help you work out how much they cost to run.

What to do

Start a new spreadsheet and follow the instructions in the diagram.

Look at the 'rating plate' on various electrical appliances and record their power rating.

Get the children to tally how long each appliance was used for daily. The should add their results to the spreadsheet table.

Questions to ask

Which appliance do you use the most?

Which appliance costs the most to run?

Which appliance costs the least to run?

Once all the results have been added, you can set a budget for the electricity bill. The children can then change the values in the Time used column and see if they can match the figure you set.

For example:

How could you get your electricity bill down to 100 pence a day?

Extra

Use a spreadsheet to do a survey of your use of water. Find out how much water a bath holds, how many baths you take and so on.

	A	B	C	D	E
1	How can we save electricity?				Pence
2			One Energy unit costs		6
3	Appliance	Power	Time used	Energy units	Cost
4		W	Minutes		p
5	Kettle	2700	70	3.2	19
6	Hair dryer	400	10	0.1	0.4
7	TV	190	240	0.8	5
8	Lamps	100	1000	1.7	10
9	Computer	100	150	0.3	2
10	Dryer	3000	180	9.0	54
11				TOTAL	89

How to set up your spreadsheet
1. Copy rows 1 to 4 as shown here.
2. Copy columns A and B as shown here.
3. Enter the Time used in column C.
4. Move to cell D5 and enter the formula =B5*C5/60/1000
This works out the electricity company's energy units.
5. Move to cell E5 and enter the formula =D5*E2
This turns the electricity company's energy units into money.
6. Highlight cells D5 to E5 and choose Copy.
7. Highlight cells D6 to E10 and choose Paste.
8. Move to cell E11 and enter =SUM(E5:E10)
This works out the total electricity bill.

IT tools

Section

2

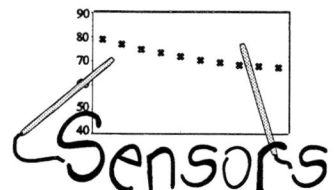

Sensors

Why sensors?

A child might point a light sensor at the window and on the computer screen she might see a rising bar gauge. Although she may not know what the sensor is responding to or be good at numbers, she has begun to explore a tool which will help her to appreciate measurement.

Measurement is a feature of all science work. With a sensor connected to your computer, your software can display the readings as a number, a bar or a time graph. Some programs can even show pictures: an aeroplane for a loud sound, a bird for the quietest sound and so on. Using sensors gives children a much better feel for measurement. The thin line in thermometers, the scales on meters hardly help understanding - they are just tools to give you numbers.

Using sensors, or 'data logging' is a focus for good science.

What you need

There are sensors to measure almost anything. You will probably want to measure temperature, sound and light levels and that may be enough. A second temperature sensor will let you compare the temperatures of two things and that is useful. A pair of light switches or light gates can time how quickly things fall, but that is where you might stop, or at least pause.

There are also sensors that measure your pulse or breathing rate and others that monitor the weather: a rotation sensor measures the wind speed and a humidity sensor can measure moisture in the air.

The software is a make-or-break item. It should allow you to display your measurements as numbers, as moving gauges and as a graph against time. It should allow you to measure for as long as you need to - be that a few minutes or a whole day. It should also let you record the readings from two sensors at the same time.

The software should automatically identify which sensors you have plugged in and it should scale the measurements as degrees, sound level or whatever. Good software can ensure that your kit does not spend its life in a cupboard.

If you have a single sensor kit and want to use it around the school a portable computer is invaluable. Most kits work with different computers - for the price of a cable and some more software.

Activities using sensors

The following double-page spreads detail some activities which work with even the most basic software. The 'pupil pages' are purely a guide to the points to make during the activity.

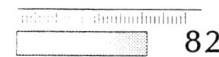 82

Bar gauge display

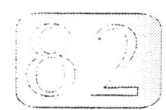

Digital display

Analogue meter display

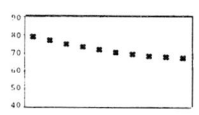

Time graph display

IT tools

Section
2

See also:
Assessment   *Page 11*
Ideas section   *Page 69*
Reference   *Page 125*

Sensor glossary

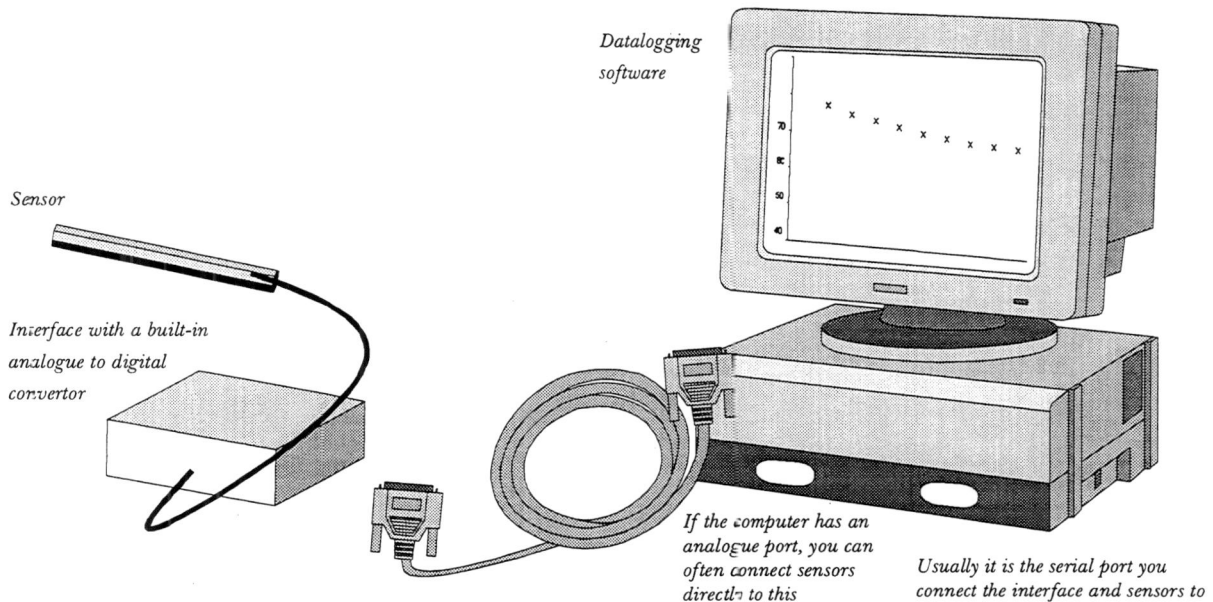

Datalogging software

Sensor

Interface with a built-in analogue to digital convertor

If the computer has an analogue port, you can often connect sensors directly to this

Usually it is the serial port you connect the interface and sensors to

Sound sensor - measures the sound level. Use it to study sound proofing or do a noise survey.

Temperature sensor - measures how hot something is. Use it to study cooling, heating, and the weather. Two sensors are almost essential for comparing things cooling.

Humidity sensor - measures the amount of water in the air. Use for monitoring the weather or the moisture in exhaled air.

Pressure sensor - measures the air pressure. Use for monitoring the weather or how pressure changes with depth of water.

Rotation sensor - measures the speed of rotation. Use for monitoring the wind speed, the speed of a motor or gears.

Real-time data logging - when you collect readings from sensors and show the readings at the same time.

Position sensor - measures the angle of movement.

Interface - a box that plugs into a computer. You need one to connect the sensors to the computer.

Data logging - collecting data from sensors. Some devices can do this away from the computer - in the playground, for example, these are called data loggers.

Data logger - a self-contained device to collect readings from sensors away from the computer. You can connect the data logger to the computer to see these readings.

Bar gauge - a way of showing how much a sensor is changing.

Time graph - a way of showing how sensor readings change over time.

Light gate / Light switch - a sensor which responds rapidly to changes in light level. Used for timing events with great accuracy.

Sensor box - a box or 'interface' you connect to the computer to collect readings from sensors.

Digital sensor - a sensor or switch that has two states, on or off. Light gates, switches and pressure pads are digital sensors.

Analogue sensor - temperature and light sensors are analogue sensors. Unlike digital sensors, these have many 'states' and can provide readings over a wide range of change.

Analogue Port - a socket on a computer where you might connect sensors or a sensor box.

Serial Port - a socket on a computer where you connect a sensor box. Your sensors connect to this box.

Analogue to digital converter - inside some sensor boxes is a microchip which converts a reading from an analogue sensor into a digital reading which the computer can understand.

Data logging software - software which records and displays the readings from sensors. Usually supplied with your data logging kit.

IT tools

Section

2

What this is about

If a cup of hot water has a higher temperature than the room, it loses heat energy to the room. In contrast, ice water, which has a lower temperature than the room, will gain heat energy from the room. Knowing the temperature of an object tells us how hot or cold something is. It allows us to predict whether it will gain or lose heat from the surroundings.

In this activity the children make predictions, collect evidence, make measurements and present their results.

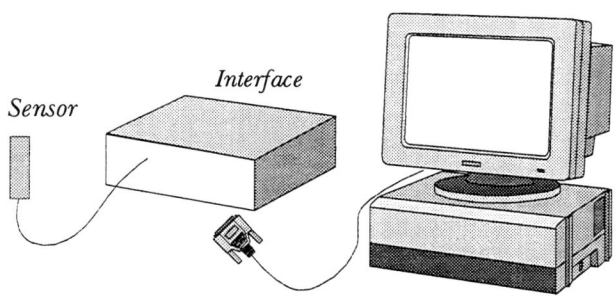

Sensor　*Interface*

You will need

Hot and cold water, boiled water (care), ice, cold drink, hot drink, warm food, a heater and a hair dryer. Also: temperature sensor, sensor box, computer cable, sensing software.

Starting points

Children should see the temperature change as a temperature probe adjusts to their hand. They should measure the temperature of warm and cold water to gain a tacit appreciation of temperature changes.

Ask the group for examples of when taking temperatures is useful.

Which things around them do they think are hotter than themselves? Which items are cooler? Get them to record their predictions in a table or thermometer diagram.

Investigate

Get the computer to display a bar gauge and large numbers. Place the tip of the temperature probe in the item you are testing. After a minute or so - i.e. when the temperature has stabilised, record the reading. Ask the children to suggest other items to measure.

They can record their results as shown opposite or attach picture cards of hot food, cold drink on a large thermometer.

Extra

At what temperature is butter easy to spread? Place some butter in a small container inside a larger container of warm water. Measure the temperature until it softens.

Taking temperatures

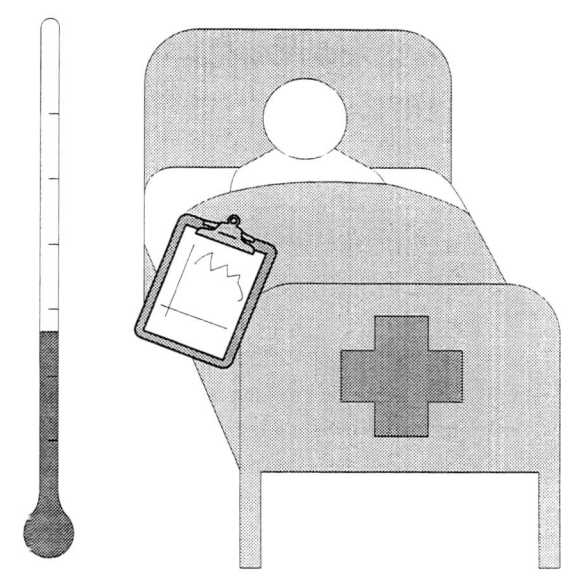

The temperature tells us how hot something is. Something with a high temperature is hot. Something with a low temperature is cold. In this activity you test some temperatures.

You need:

Hot and cold items. Computer, printer and the temperature sensor.

Investigate

1. Get the computer ready to measure temperature.
2. Get the computer to show your readings.
3. Take the temperature of:

   Your hands

   Hot water

   Cold water

   Ice

   A hot drink

   A cold drink

   The room

   The air outside the window

   The air above a radiator

   The air below a radiator

4. Record your findings

Questions

1. What was the hottest?
2. What was the coldest?
3. Put your results on a thermometer chart.

Extra

What is the best temperature for butter to spread?

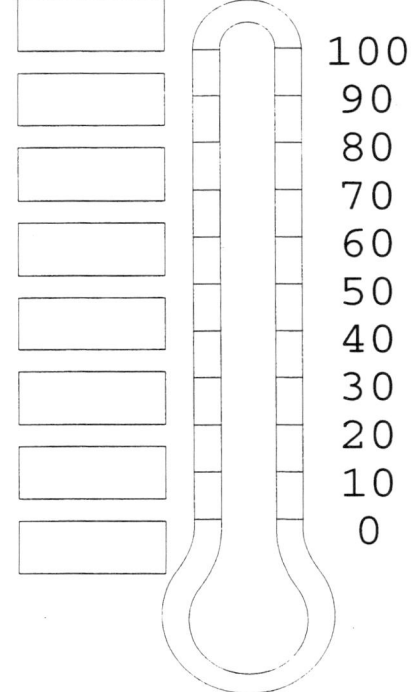

Item tested	Temperature
Hot water	
Cold water	
Warm food	
Hands	
Ice	
....	

Keeping baby warm

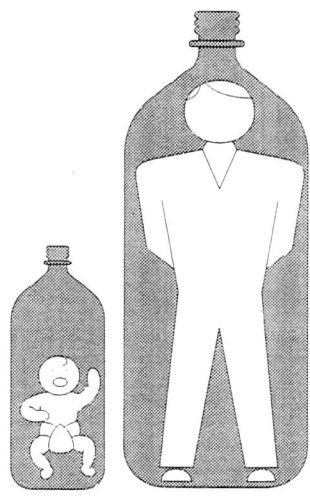

What this is about

Babies and adults are warmer than their surroundings and constantly lose heat to it. Other things being equal, how quickly they lose heat depends on their size and the surrounding temperature.

The explanation is not so important at this level but the more skin you have contact with the surroundings the faster you lose heat. Animals huddle or curl up to expose less 'skin'. A baby has more skin for its size than an adult and it loses heat easily. Insulating materials, such as blankets, slow down the loss of heat.

In this activity the children make a fair test of a baby and an adult and make measurements using sensors. They compare their results and draw a conclusion.

You will need

Large and small metal containers decorated as 'baby' and 'adult' in a bowl or tray and hand hot water. Temperature sensor, interface, computer cable, software and printer.

Starting points

Ask the group how they would dress a small baby for a visit to the park. Would the baby need to have more covering than themselves? Is a baby more sensitive to cold? Does a baby get cold faster than an adult? How might we investigate this?

Investigate

The children can use temperature sensors to compare the cooling of containers filled with hot water. They might record for about 15 minutes.

If you have one temperature sensor they can do two separate runs, one for each container. To help compare the two graphs, ensure that the starting temperatures are similar. Place or trace one time graph over the other. The small container of hot water will cool faster than the large container. It will show a lower final temperature and the graph will fall more steeply.

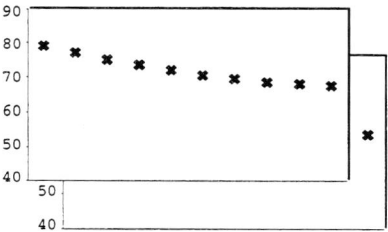

Extra

Repeat the investigation using two baby containers, wrap one of these in a blanket.

IT tools

Section

2

Keeping baby warm

Who do you think will get cold first - a baby or an adult?

You need

Care! You will be using hot water. Make sure it does not get knocked over.

Hot water, a large and a small container. Computer, printer and the temperature sensor.

Investigate

1. Get the computer ready to measure temperature.

2. Fill small and large containers with hot water. These are the baby and adult.

3. Get the computer to draw a time graph as they cool down.

4. Stop recording after fifteen minutes. Now print the graph.

Questions

1. What was the temperature of your baby after fifteen minutes?

2. What was the temperature of the adult after fifteen minutes?

3. Look at your graphs. Which loses heat faster, a baby or an adult?

4. Where do you think the baby's heat went?

Extra:

Does wrapping a baby in a blanket help to keep it warm?

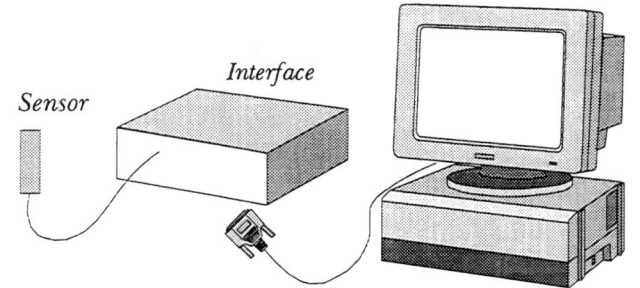

Sensor

Interface

What this is about

Hot things cool because they lose heat to their surroundings. We can help them to cool by making the surroundings cooler (by blowing) or by conducting heat away with a spoon. The greater the difference in temperature between an object and its surroundings, the faster it will cool. A spoon left in a drink will help cool it by conducting the heat into the surroundings. If we pour a drink between two cups we provide a bigger area for the drink to lose heat from.

In this activity the children make measurements using sensors. They draw a conclusion from their results.

You will need

A plastic cup of hand hot water in a tray, temperature sensor, interface, computer cable, software.

Starting points

How long would a very hot drink take to cool? How could they make the drink cool down faster?

Investigate

Your hot water should be at a safe temperature. The children should measure the temperature of a cup of water as it cools. They can compare this with a second cup where they try to speed up the cooling. The children might try one idea at a time: blowing on the surface, placing the cup in the draught of a fan, pouring the drink between two cups, leaving a spoon in the drink, placing it near a window or placing it in a dish of cold water. Record for about 15 minutes.

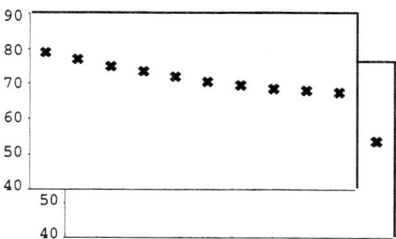

If you have one temperature sensor they can do two separate runs, one for each container. To help compare the graphs, see that the starting temperatures are similar.

Making your hot drink cool

How can you make a hot drink cool down faster? Which way is best?

You need

A cup, hot water and a bowl. Computer, printer and the temperature sensor.

Investigate

Care! You will be using hot water.

1. Get the computer ready to measure temperature.

2. Make two hot drinks

3. Get the computer to draw a time graph

4. Try to make one drink cool down faster by blowing on it.

5. Stop the recording after fifteen minutes. Now print the graph.

Questions

1. What was the temperature of your freshly made drink?

2. What was its temperature after fifteen minutes?

3. What did you do to make the second drink cool down faster?

4. What was its temperature after fifteen minutes?

5. Where do you think the heat in your drinks went to?

Extra

See if can find a better way to make your drink cool down.

What is the temperature of a hot drink ready for drinking?

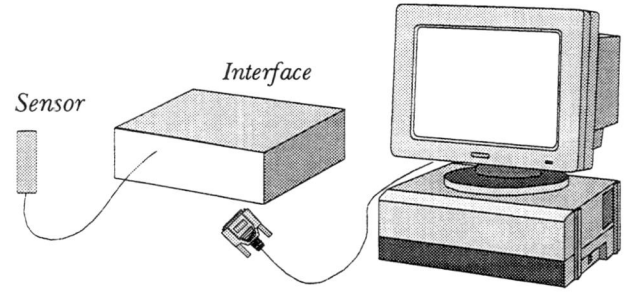

Sensor

Interface

Can you trust your ears?

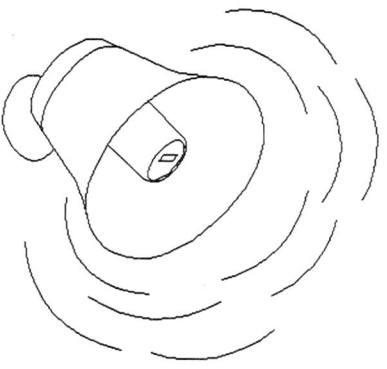

Materials which set up vibrations in the air make sound. These vibrations are little 'puffs' of higher air pressure followed by gaps of lower air pressure. The bigger these 'puffs' are, the louder is the sound. Loudness is measured with a sound meter or sound sensor. The unit for measuring sound is the decibel, named after Bell, the inventor of the telephone. A 'Bel' is too large a unit for everyday use so we use the decibel.

The pitch of a sound, which is how high or low a sound is, must not be confused with loudness. To measure the pitch of a sound you need an oscilloscope or frequency meter.

In this activity the children guess how loud sounds are and compare their guesses with the sound sensor. The activity aims to highlight the value of using measuring instruments.

You will need

Aim at a balance of percussion, string, wind and electronic sound makers: musical instruments, a ticking clock, elastic bands, spoons, scissors, tuning forks, containers filled with rice or paper clips, blocks of wood, a drum, a radio and so on. Interface, cable, sound sensor, software.

Starting points

Do your folks ask you to 'turn down the noise?' Does 'loud' depend on what the sound is?

Can they use their ears to find the loudest and the quietest sound makers? How could they record how loud the sounds are?

See how quiet the group can be.

Investigate

Get the software to show the sound level as a number or bar gauge. The sensor is very sensitive and picks up most sounds. How can they measure the sound from the sound maker and not something else in the room?

Where should they place sound source and sensor?

How do their guesses compare with the sound sensor?

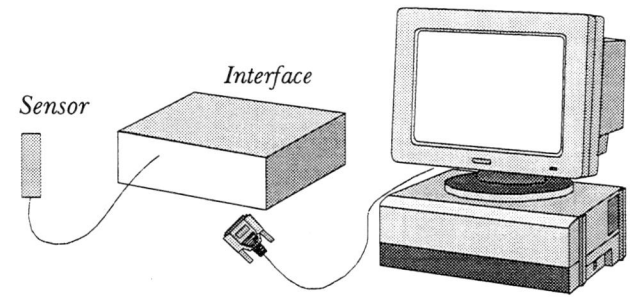

Sensor *Interface*

Can you trust your ears?

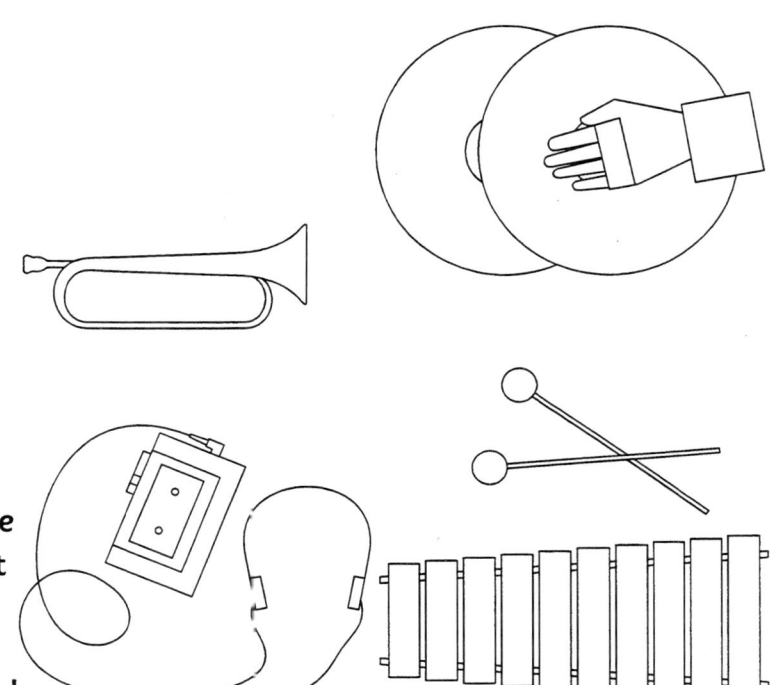

Which sound makers make the loudest sounds? Can you trust your ears to decide? In this activity you will use the computer to measure how loud sounds are.

You need

Sound makers. Computer and the sound sensor.

Investigate

1. Which sounds will you test? Will you play the sound makers 'hard' or 'soft'?

2. Try the sound makers and decide which sounds are quiet and which ones are loud.

3. Test each sound using the sound sensor.

4. Record the sound level in your table.

Questions

1. Did you and the others agree on what was 'loud' and 'quiet'?

2. Sort the sound makers into order, loudest first

3. Make a sound level scale with the numbers from 0 to 100. Mark it to show Quiet, Loud, and Very loud.

4. Do your ears and the sound sensor disagree?

Extra

If you drop something, does it make more noise if you drop it from higher up?

Type of sound	How sound is made	Quiet or Loud	Sound level
Drum			
Flute			
Guitar			
Talking			
Ticking clock			

IT tools

Section

2

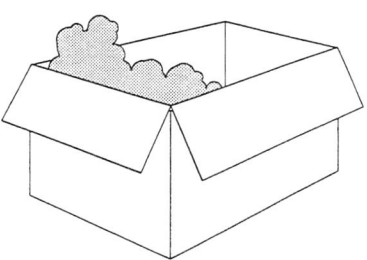

Noise is sound being a nuisance or causing ear damage but sound proofing against this is difficult. This is because all sorts of materials vibrate and transmit sound. Having sound absorbers, such as carpets and curtains helps to absorb sound. Also, when a sound is made the vibrations in the air cause surfaces to vibrate and to reflect sound. Materials such as insulating felt and foam do not reflect sound well nor do they vibrate very well. In contrast a sheet of metal or wood does vibrate well and does not insulate sound well.

In this activity children 'do an investigation' and use a sound sensor to measure sound levels.

You will need

A consistent sound source such as a buzzer, bell or tape recording. A few of these materials: cotton wool, foam, cork, newspapers, card, wood, polystyrene, an inflated balloon, a cushion, a blanket, thick or padded clothing; cardboard egg-boxes. Also: computer, monitor, sound sensor, interface, cable and software.

Starting points

When is sound useful? When is sound called music? When is sound called noise?

How do they shut out sound when there is a lot of noise next door?

Investigate

Make a steady sound. Measure its sound level with the sensor covered with different materials in turn. Or place the sound sensor in a shoe box and line the box with various materials. Note: Sound can easily 'leak' around the sound insulator.

IT tools

Section

2

Can you make ear muffs for teacher?

Your teacher can't get to sleep. She would like some ear muffs - but what should she make them from? Use the sound sensor to find the best material to stop sounds.

You need

A sound maker, materials to stop sound such as clothing, a blanket, a cushion, egg boxes, cork, polystyrene. Computer and the sound sensor.

Investigate

1. Decide which sound maker you will use. It needs to make a loud, steady sound.

2. Make a sound and record the sound level.

3. Choose a material that might stop sound, for example use a blanket.

4. Put the material around the sound sensor and record how much sound gets through.

5. Try the other materials.

Questions

1. Which material is the best at stopping sound?

2. Do the sound proofers have anything in common?

Extra

Does twice the thickness of the material stop the sounds any better?

Material	Sound level (before)	Sound level (after)	Difference in sound level
Blanket			
Folded blanket			
Egg boxes			

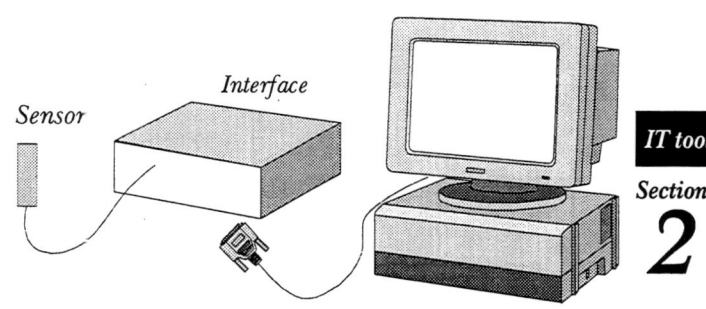

Sensor *Interface*

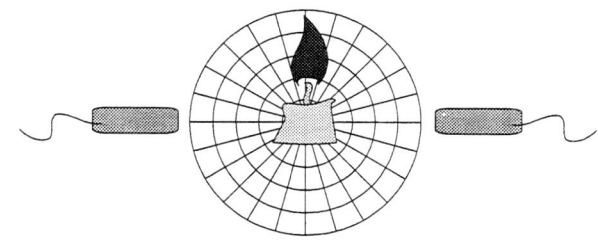

We need light to see things and light comes from something that is hot or burning. A torch or light bulb has tungsten wire which glows when hot. Candles produce light by burning chemicals. Some light sources are more directional than others.

In this activity the children use a light sensor to take light level readings. They 'do an investigation' where they need to make sure their tests are fair. For example, they need to control how far away the light source is.

You will need

A candle, some torches, a torch without a reflector, tungsten lamp, fluorescent strip light and daylight. Light sensor, interface, cable, software, computer and monitor.

Starting points

How many ways can we get light? Can you put them in order of brightness? Why do scientists measure light levels instead of guessing them?

Investigate

Use the light sensor at the same distance from the source. Stray light will affect your readings, so place a tube made of card around the sensor.

Extra

Does light come from the back and sides of a light source? Place a candle in the middle of a circle and take readings around it. Light spreads out in all directions from a light source. This is why we use reflectors and lamp shades.

IT tools

Section

2

Which light is the brightest?

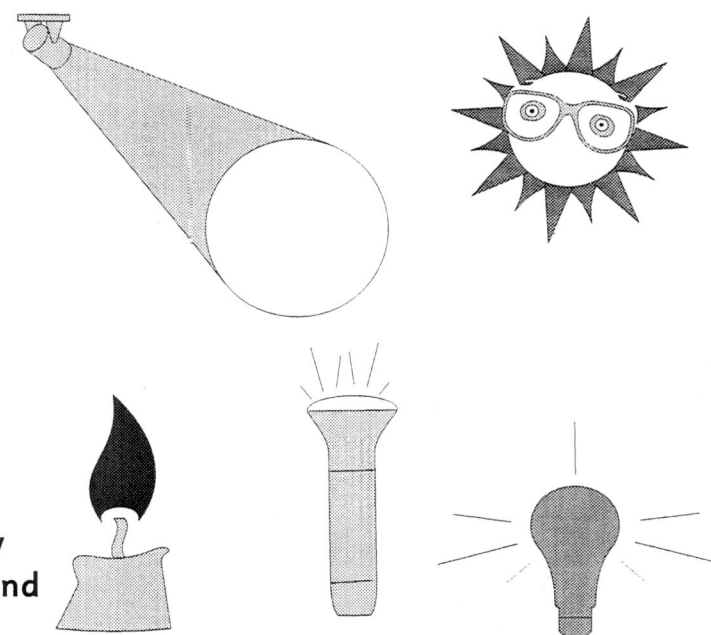

The light sensor can measure how bright light is. You will use it to find the brightest light source.

You need

A candle, torch, torch without a reflector, tungsten lamp, fluorescent strip light and daylight. Computer and the light sensor.

Investigate

1. Can you stop the light in the room from getting to the light sensor?
2. How close will you hold the light sensor to the lights?
3. Test some light sources, to find the brightest.
4. Record your light level readings.

Questions

1. Put the lights into order.
2. Which light would be the best for reading in the day time?
3. Which light would be the best for reading at night time?

Extra

Does light come from the back and the sides of your lights?

Light Source	Light level
Torch	
Strip light	
Sunlight	
Tungsten light	
Candle	

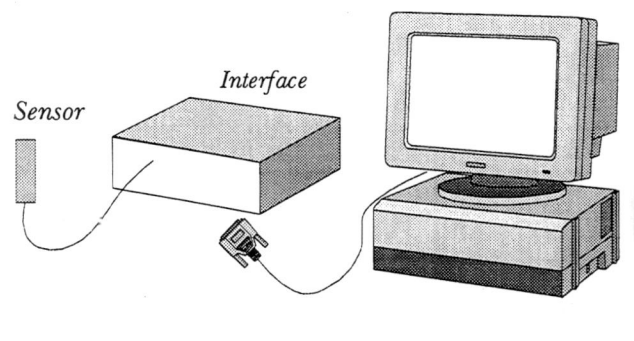

Sensor   *Interface*

IT tools

Section

2

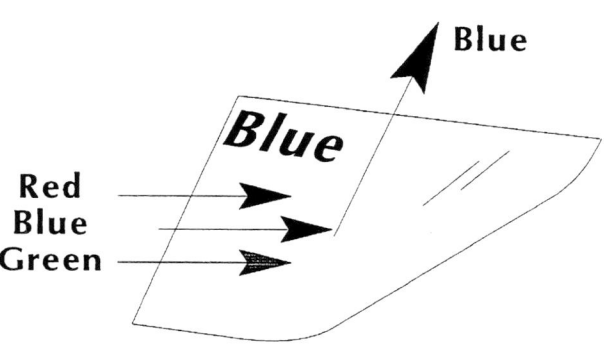

Most substances reflect some light and that is why we can see them. White light is a mixture of many colours mixed together. When white light shines on say, a blue fabric, the fabric reflects blue and absorbs every colour except blue. Similarly a red fabric reflects red and absorbs all other colours.

A black fabric absorbs all the colours of white light and reflects little light back. A white fabric absorbs little white light and reflects most colours back. Shiny fabrics reflect even more light back. Fluorescent fabrics, often worn by cyclists, temporarily store and emit the light shining on them.

In this activity the children use a light sensor to take light level readings. They 'do an investigation' where they need to make sure their tests are fair. For example, they need to control how they illuminate the fabrics and how far away the light source is.

You will need

A desk lamp, fabrics of different colour, reflective materials, shiny and dull fabrics in the same colour. Light sensor, interface, cable and software.

Starting points

How can we be safe when walking and cycling? What colour clothes get us noticed? Don't animals try to camouflage themselves? Can we compare the brightness of clothes by eye?

Investigate

Use a desk lamp to illuminate the fabrics. Direct the sensor at each fabric and fix the sensor into position.

Extra

Children can test their fabrics under poor lighting conditions. They may find some fabrics change their position in the 'league table'. For example, a shiny fabric will not reflect much light under poor lighting.

Which colour should a cyclist wear?

Which colour do you think is the brightest?

The light sensor can measure brightness. In this activity you will use it to compare the colours of clothing.

You need:

Fabrics of different colour, shiny and dull fabrics in the same colour. Computer and the light sensor.

Investigate

1. Get the computer to measure the light level.
2. Test each of the fabrics.
3. Record your readings.

Questions

1. Put the fabrics into order - put the brightest first.
2. Which fabrics would be safest to wear?
3. Say how you made a fair test of the fabrics.

Extra

Suppose you were riding a cycle in the evening. Do you think your clothes would look as bright? Do another experiment to see.

Fabric	Light level
Black	
Yellow cotton	
Yellow plastic	
Day-Glo plastic	
White	

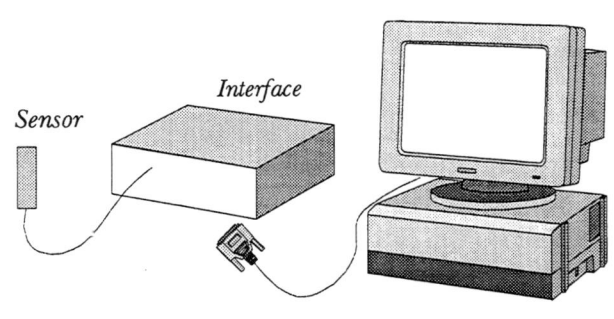

IT tools

Section

2

Why control?

Control technology is a tool that allows you to create an automated system. It allows you to do those 'techie' things, like use the computer to control some traffic lights, or control a buggy or run a 'washing machine'. It is fairly straightforward to do and potentially good fun too.

Computer control activities can be thoroughly absorbing and relevant to IT, technology and science curricula. For example, the children identify a need and analyse a situation. They create a solution to a problem and predict the outcome. They also learn about automation and sequencing computer instructions. Control technology is obviously a tool for learning.

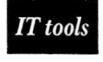

Section 2

See also:

Assessment	Page 11
Ideas section	Page 69
Resources section	Page 125

Control

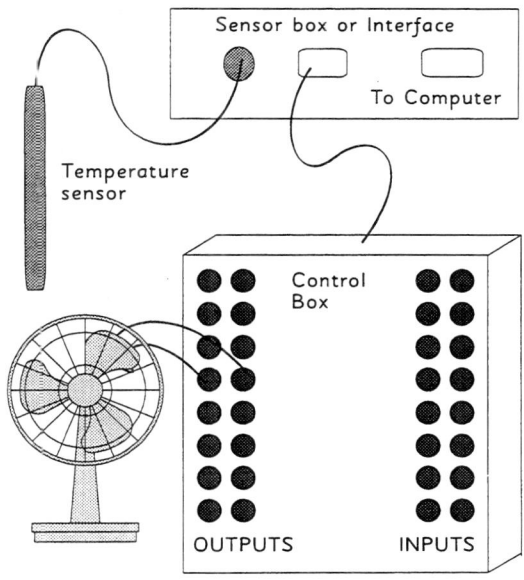

Sensor box or Interface

To Computer

Temperature sensor

Control Box

OUTPUTS   INPUTS

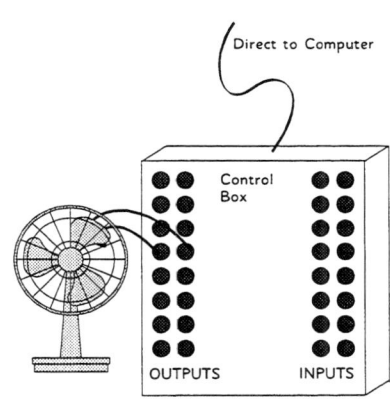

Direct to Computer

Control Box

OUTPUTS   INPUTS

What you need

If you have all you need for control work, the whole business is fairly straightforward. The hard bit is collecting together the 'kit' you need. It gets harder the more time that passes since you ordered your kit, or went on a course.

To do control, you need to connect three key items. First you need models to control. The models have output devices such as lights and motors. They may even have sensors or input devices provide useful information. Second, you need to connect them to the computer through a control box. Third you need software to send messages to the control box.

For example, if you want to switch on a fan when the room gets too hot you would need a motor for the fan and a sensor to measure the temperature.

Your fan can be a propeller blade and a motor. The motor's wires go to the control box. Or you can make the fan with Lego or just buy a battery-operated one.

The control box has a set of input and output sockets. It may also have special sockets for motors and sensors. Small lights or LEDs on the box tell you when the sockets are active - which helps in finding whether a fault lies in your model (the fan) or somewhere else in the system.

You plug the control box straight into your computer, or plug it into a sensor box plugged into the computer. For example, the BBC computer has printer and user port sockets and many control boxes connect here. You can upgrade Archimedes and Nimbus computers to have printer and user port sockets so you can connect the control box to these. Alternatively, you may be able to plug a control box into your sensor box.

Modern control boxes connect to a different socket on the machine altogether, this is the 'serial port' and you should find at least one on every PC, Macintosh and Archimedes. (Some Archimedes' need to have 'serial chips' fitted).

There are now so many systems, and so many ways to combine the equipment that I would recommend you write up or better, photograph how your system fits together when you get it working. Keep these pictures, and pictures of successful projects with the control kit - it helps!

IT tools

Section

2

What you need - continued

A few suppliers will sell you ready-made models to control - traffic lights, mounted motors, pictures with lights and things built into them. Beginners will appreciate these. (See under Control Accessories in the reference section.)

The final item in your control kit is the software. Once you have run this and set it up to match your system you should be ready for business.

The children type in or click-on 'key words' like SWITCHON [1 2] or REPEAT 3 [SWITCHON [1 2] and build up a series of commands to control their models. The software also allows then to switch on say, a fan when a special condition occurs - for example, IF SWITCH=ON THEN SWITCHON 1 will switch something on if you press a switch. Modern equipment and software allows them to use analogue sensors, such as temperature sensors in their control systems. For example, they might enter IF TEMPERATURE IS ABOVE 30 THEN SWITCHON 1 to switch on a fan when the temperature rises above 30 degrees.

Control without wires

There are some easier routes to control which do not involve control boxes. For example, the Logo language helps create a feel for giving commands. This is the program where you type commands such as FORWARD 20 and draw a line on the screen - many control programs are Logo-like so Logo is a good starting point. Logowriter (from Valiant) is an interesting version of Logo - adding stories, pictures and text to Logo activities.

Then there are programs that simulate control. The children might give instructions to the computer to say, load an elephant onto a lorry or load crates onto a ship. In one the children use the keyboard to direct a Teddy round a playground. See under Control in the reference section.

Children can also use a Robot such as Pip, Pixie or Roamer - motorised buggies that move forward and turn using a built in keyboard. These can tour the classroom, or visit different places on a large picture of say, a farm. These are easier to understand. See the Reference section for the details on robots.

Contexts for control

Computer control activities will find a place in science and technology topics. For example,

In an electricity topic you can wire up traffic lights.

In a **machines** theme you can develop a buggy, a washing machine, a car park barrier or a bridge that opens and closes.

In a **weather** topic you can make a device which opens and closes a window depending on the temperature. Or you could develop a device, which always faces the sun even when the sun 'moves' across the sky.

In a **living things** topic you can make a device that counts birds arriving at a bird table. Or devise a machine to meter out bird food.

In an **ourselves** topic you can use control technology to mimic the control systems of the human body. A machine might move in response to sound and light. Or you could make a baby incubator and keep it at a steady temperature.

Control activities

The problems on the pages that follow can be solved using control technology. The first two problems are easier and merely involve switching lights on and off. The next two use analogue sensors and show you how to create a more refined control system.

Control glossary

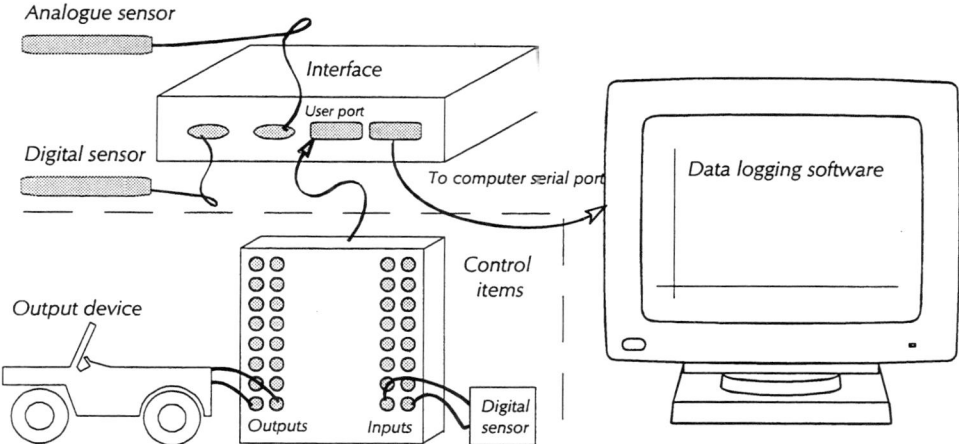

Buzzer - a type of output device you can use in say, an alarm system.

Control box - a box or interface which allows you to switch on lights, motors and buzzers. The box will also have sockets for sensors and switches. It plugs into the computer and a power source.

Control module - a mini-control unit allowing you to use devices which play music or display numbers.

Control software - the programs you use to read information from sensors and switch devices on and off. Each control program has its own dialect of the control language. You use this language to write programs for control systems.

Digital sensor - a sensor or switch which has two states, on or off. For example, a light sensor responds to light or dark, a pressure mat responds to pressing on it.

Hydraulic pump - a device which will pump or squirt water. You can use this to automatically water plants and for all sorts of mischievous purposes.

Interface - a box that plugs into a computer.

LED - or light emitting diode. These are used in indicator lamps in all sorts of electronic equipment. They need only a little power to light them.

Light switch or Light gate - a digital sensor which responds to something covering it. Used to sense when it gets dark, time events or to count objects moving along a conveyor belt.

Motor - a type of output device you can use to work a model.

Push Switch - a switch that responds to momentary pressure. Use like a bell-push or like the push control on a pelican crossing.

Pressure mat - a switch that responds to pressure. Use one under a mat to signal when someone has entered a shop. Or use one to get the computer to measure children's reaction times.

Proximity switch - a switch that switches on or off when close to another object. A reed switch is a type of proximity switch. When a magnet passes close to it, it triggers a response.

Ram-rod - a device, like a syringe barrel, which moves in or out when you switch it on. You can use this for automatically opening a model window or door.

Sensor - sensors can be digital or analogue types. Modern control systems let you use analogue sensors such as a temperature sensor. Using your control program, you can measure the temperature and get say, a fan to switch on or off at a certain temperature.

Sensor box - a box ('interface') you connect to the computer to collect readings from sensors. You can plug control boxes into some sensor boxes.

Serial port - a socket on a computer where you can connect control boxes and sensor boxes.

Temperature sensor - the temperature sensor in your control kit is probably a digital temperature sensor. This means it doesn't tell you the temperature - it just sends out an 'on' signal when it is hot.

Tilt switch - a mercury-filled switch that switches on or off when tilted. Use one to set off an alarm when you open a desk.

Toggle switch - a two-position switch like a domestic light switch.

User port - a socket on a computer or an interface where you can connect control boxes.

IT tools

Section

2

Belisha beacon

Make a light flash like a Belisha beacon.

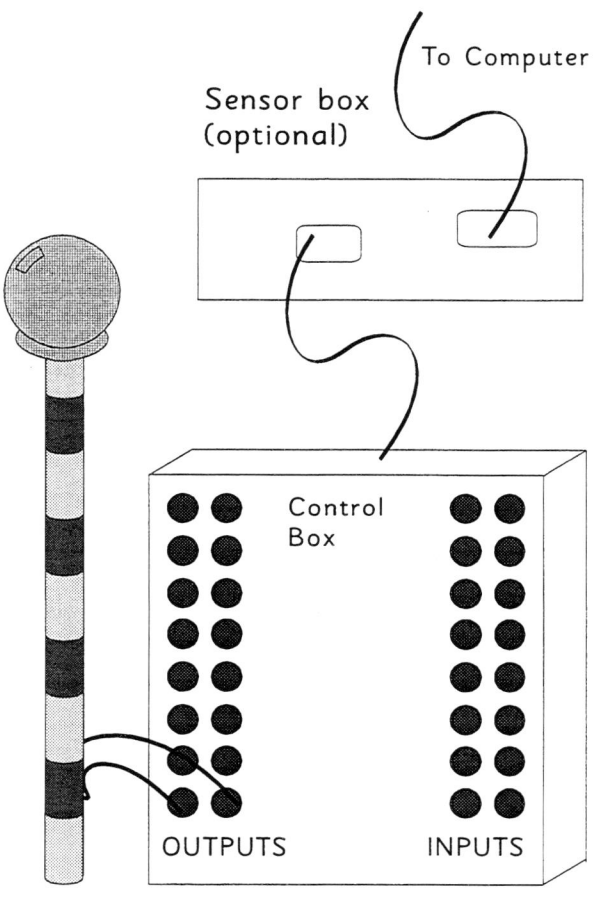

To Computer

Sensor box (optional)

Control Box

OUTPUTS

INPUTS

What this is about

The children make a control system to simulate a simple traffic light. They create, test and store a sequence of instructions to make it work.

Starting points

How many times does a beacon flash in a minute? How long should the light stay on?

What to do

Connect the Control box to the computer or sensor box. Connect a lamp to the Control box.

Next, run your control program and type in something like this:

```
REPEAT
SWITCH ON 1
WAIT 5
SWITCH OFF 1
AGAIN
```

Does this work? If so, you can turn it into a procedure:

```
BUILD beacon
REPEAT
SWITCH ON 1
WAIT 5
SWITCH OFF 1
AGAIN
END
```

To run this procedure type:
```
DO beacon
```

Extra

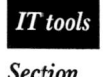

IT tools

Section

2

Make two flashing beacons, one flashing after the other.

Traffic light

Make some traffic lights.

What this is about

The children make a control system to simulate traffic lights. They create a sequence of instructions to make it work. The final part introduces them to using the computer for decision making.

Starting point

What is the order for red, amber and green on the traffic lights?

What to do

Connect the Control box to the computer or sensor box. Connect three lamps, red, amber and green to the Control box. Then you will need to write a program to get them to come on in the following order: red, red and amber, green then amber.

Run your control program and type in something like this:

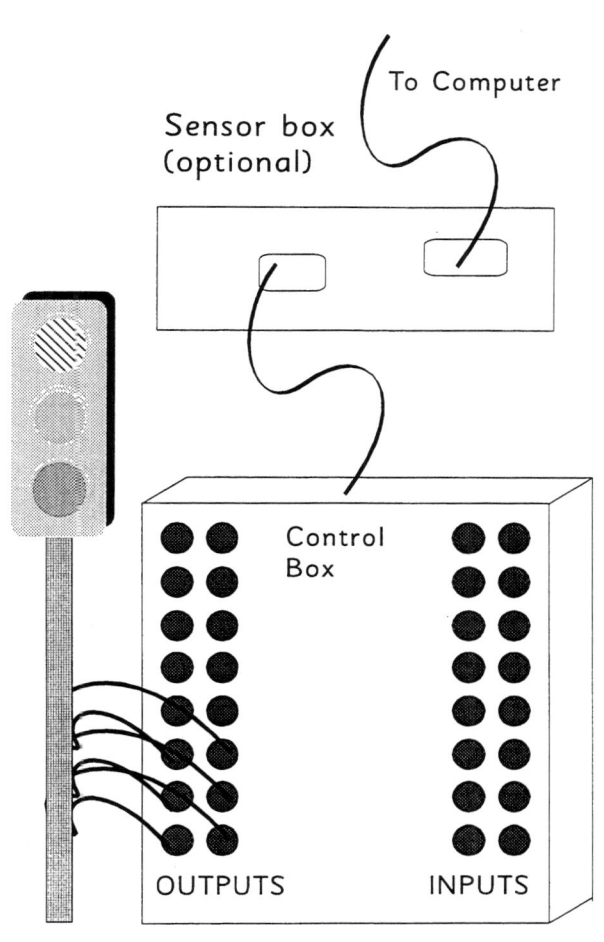

```
BUILD traffic
REPEAT
SWITCH ON 1
WAIT 5 (red stays on a while)
SWITCH ON 2
SWITCH OFF 1
SWITCH OFF 2
SWITCH ON 3
WAIT 5 (green stays on a while)
SWITCH OFF 3
SWITCH ON 2
SWITCH OFF 2
AGAIN
END
```

To run this procedure type:
```
DO traffic
```

Extra

Make the lights stay red when you press a button to cross the road. Hint: Add a line that reads, IF INPUT 1 IS ON THEN WAIT 10 in the right place.

IT tools

Section

2

Cooling Fan

The temperature is rising! Switch on a cooling fan when the temperature gets too high.

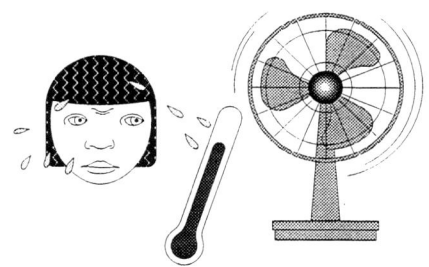

What this is about

The children make a control system which can measure temperature and power a fan. They create, test and store a sequence of instructions to make it work.

Starting points

What can you use to measure the temperature?

What should happen if the temperature is too high?

What temperature would you say is too high?

What to do

Connect a motor or fan to the Control box. Connect the Control box to the Sensor box. Connect a temperature sensor to the Sensor box. Connect the Sensor box to the computer.

Use a temperature sensor to measure the temperature. When the temperature reaches 25 degrees, switch on a fan. Get a desk lamp to warm the temperature sensor. Place the fan near the tip of the sensor. The fan will start when the temperature rises above 25 degrees.

Run your control program and type in a procedure, something like this:

```
BUILD coolme
REPEAT
IF TEMPERATURE IS ABOVE 25 THEN
SWITCH ON 5
AGAIN
END
SAVE
```

To run the procedure type:
```
DO coolme
```

Extra

What should the fan do when the room is cool? Get the fan to switch off when the temperature drops by adding this line to your program:
IF TEMPERATURE IS BELOW 25
THEN SWITCH OFF 5

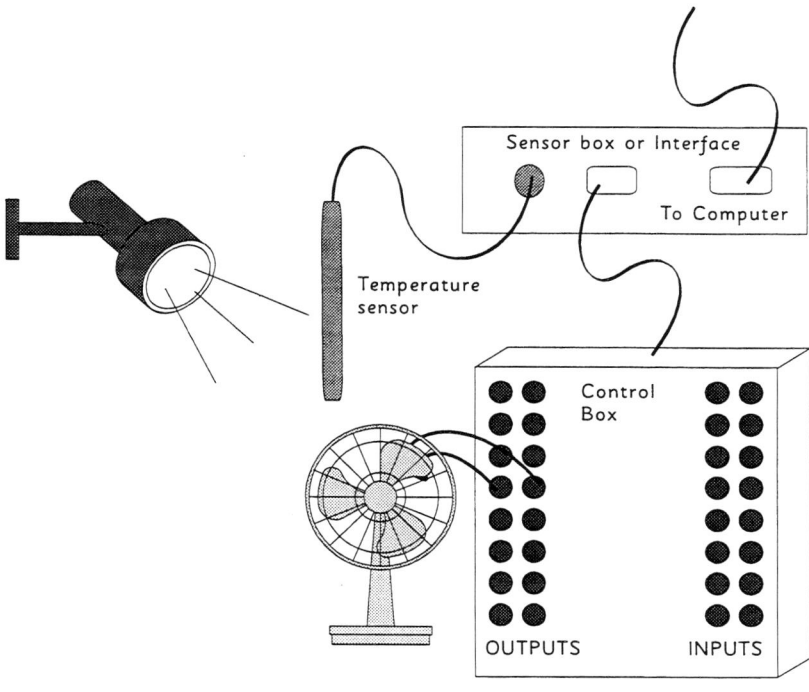

IT tools

Section

2

Automatic porch light

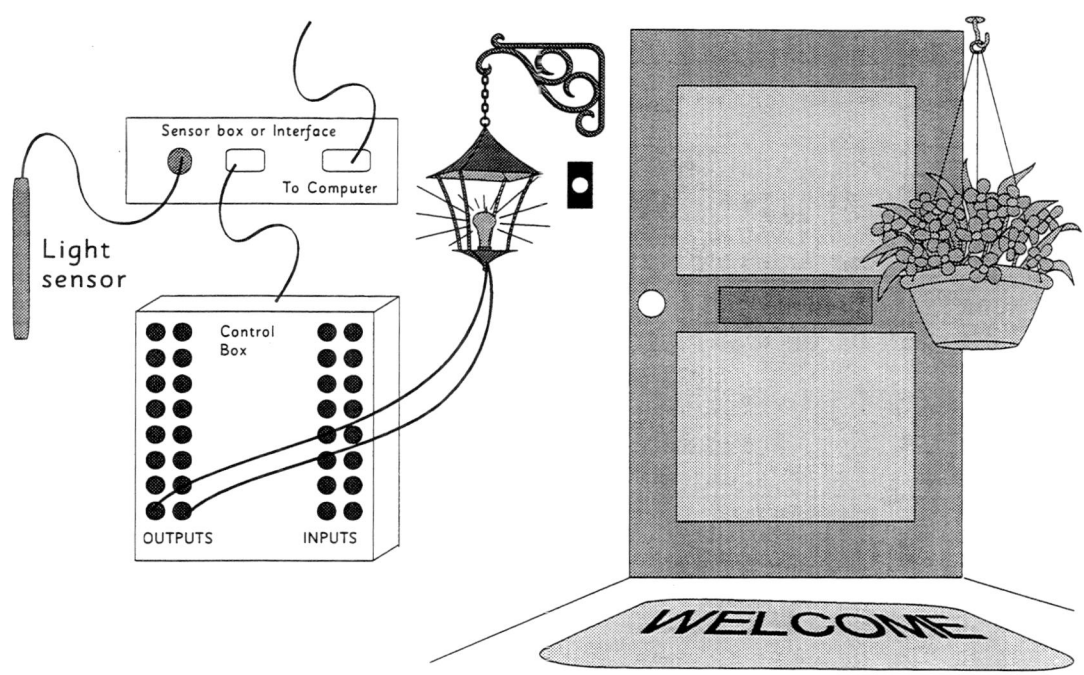

You want your front door light to come on at night and go off in the day.

What this is about

The children make a control system which can measure light and power a lamp. They create, test and store a sequence of instructions to make it work.

Starting points

What will you use to detect whether it is day or night?

At what light level should the light switch on? Above 60 or above 40?

At what light level should the light switch off? Below 60 or below 40?

What to do

Connect the Control box to the Sensor box. Connect the Sensor box to the computer. Connect a lamp to the Control box. Connect a light sensor to the Sensor box. Display the light level to answer the questions above.

Run your control program and type in a procedure, something like this:
```
REPEAT
IF LIGHT IS ABOVE 50 THEN SWITCH
ON 1
IF LIGHT IS BELOW 50 THEN SWITCH
OFF 1
AGAIN
```

Does this work? If so, you can build this into a procedure:
```
BUILD porch
REPEAT
IF LIGHT IS ABOVE 50 THEN SWITCH
ON 1
IF LIGHT IS BELOW 50 THEN SWITCH
OFF 1
AGAIN
END
```

To run this procedure type:
```
DO porch
```

Extra

Your automatic light is wasting electricity! You want the light to come on only when you arrive home at night.

IT tools

Section

2

Word processing

Word processing is more than just typing - it is a way of improving the quality of written work. It allows children to jot ideas on-screen and develop them. It allows them to rethink finished work and even then refine it. Because word processing allows children to improve their work, they do. For as long as writing is part of learning, the need for children to have access to this powerful technology will remain.

There is a hidden bonus too. With a computer screen as their focus, children can work together and discuss their task more freely than they could before. Pen and paper certainly have their role, but as the medium for collaborative work the word processor excels.

Children have a lot to document in science. They would be unusually fortunate to have sufficient access to computers to always use the word processor. The ideas in this book take this into account. They suggest 'quality not quantity' - that is, they use the word processor for tasks which have a real purpose, are reflective or are more alive.

The children might also use the word processor as a table to record their results - something which younger children will find much easier to do than use a paper table. Remember too, that if they have access to ready-made pictures on disc, they can use pictures, such as weather symbols, in a results table.

Children might write leaflets, advertisements, newsletters and stories. They can make a poster on 'saving energy' or write a Which report on different metals. They might 'just' plan an experiment or 'just' write a report. But, to help them, you can prime the computer with prompt questions such as: what are you trying to find out? Why do you think that happened? What have you leant from this?'

In the Ideas section you will find many more such examples. This section highlights a number of interesting ways of using a word processor.

IT tools

Section

2

See also:
Ideas section *page 69*
Software *page 126*

Word processor glossary

Block - a section of writing you have selected to format or move elsewhere.

Box - a rather ugly way of emphasising headings.

Centred - where you put the writing exactly in the middle of a line. Useful for headings and sub headings.

Change (Replace) - a feature which allows you to change any word or phrase to another. For example you can use it to change the name of a person called Fred to Frederick, all the way through your work. A useful feature in a longer piece of writing.

Copy - where you can copy a section of writing in the work to save you retyping it.

Cut - where you can remove a section of writing from the work. You may paste it back elsewhere in the work or even paste it into another program.

Find (Search) - to find a word or phrase. Useful for finding your place in a longer piece of writing.

Font - a feature which allows you to change the style of the letters from say, plain to decorative.

Format - where you can change the letter size, style or font.

Object - a strange but useful feature where you can place a photo, picture or graph on your page.

Paste - where you can replace a previously cut or copied section of writing back into the work.

Select - where you can choose a section of writing. For example, you might select a sentence to put it in a bolder type.

Size - where you can change the size of the lettering from small to large - for example, in headlines.

Style - where you can change the lettering style to bold, italic or bold and italic.

Tab - a special key on the keyboard which inserts a long space. It allows you to line up columns of words or numbers although the 'Table' feature does this better.

Underline - a rather dated way of emphasising headings and side headings.

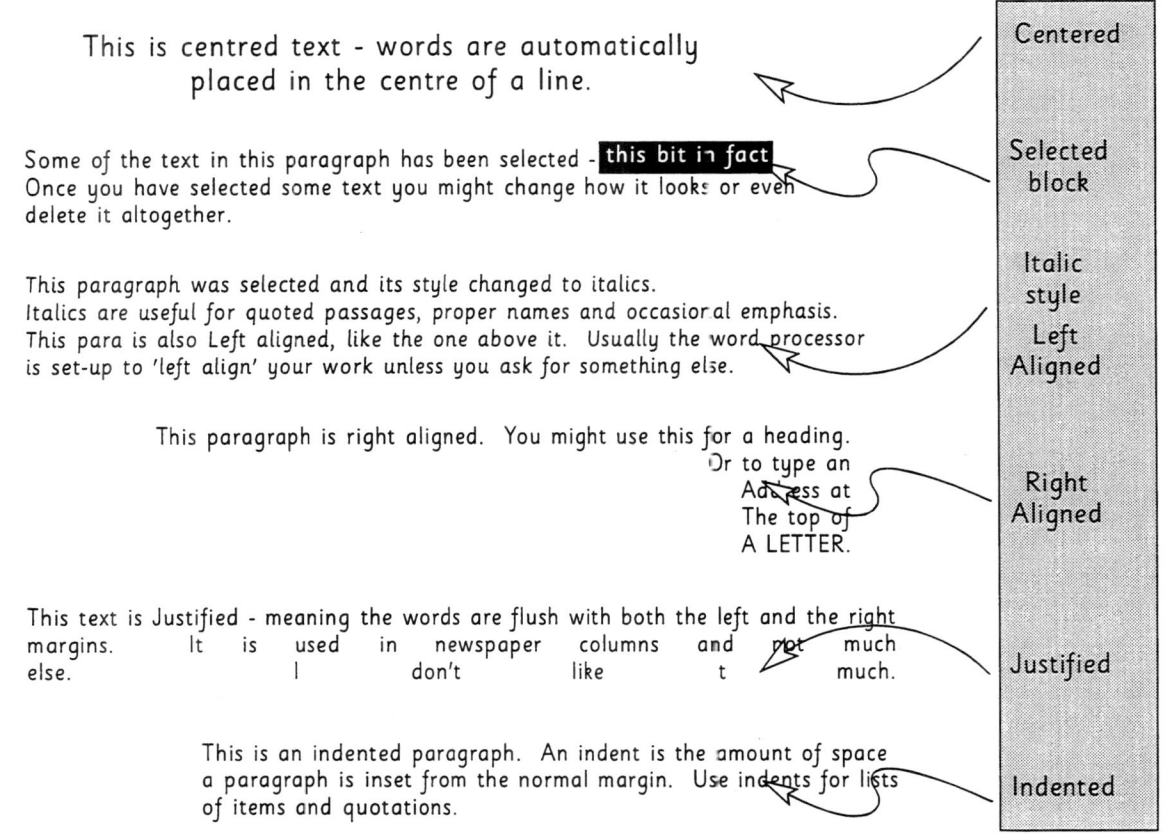

IT tools

Section

2

Word processing ideas

Making posters and advertisements

Children might use a word processor to prepare a poster on the moon, space travel, safety at home, healthy eating, keeping fit or pollution. They might for example, do some 'research' on aluminium metal and then prepare a poster advertising its features.

You will need a word processor that lets you use pictures and large type.

Writing reports

Children can write about their investigations. Most word processor programs will allow them to add graphs, and pictures to their work. Some will even allow them to add clips of video.

Missing words exercise

You can use the word processor to make a 'missing words exercise'. Using your word processor you type in the text, remove a few words and leave spaces for them. These exercises help focus attention on the written word.

> The Water Cycle.
> ⬛?⬛ moves from the sea to the ⬛?⬛ and from the air to the ⬛?⬛ in an everlasting ⬛?⬛.
> ⬛?⬛ or snow in the ⬛?⬛ ――― by the heat from the ⬛?⬛. This water ⬛?⬛ to form ⬛?⬛ and lakes. It eventually finds its way to the ⬛?⬛.
> The ⬛?⬛ warms the sea and this ⬛?⬛ water ⬛?⬛ which saturates the ⬛?⬛. Eventually, the ⬛?⬛ vapour becomes part of the ⬛?⬛. The clouds ⬛?⬛ high in the sky where the air is ⬛?⬛. The water vapour ⬛?⬛ to form ⬛?⬛.
> If it gets very ⬛?⬛ the clouds freeze to make ⬛?⬛ or ice.
> When it ⬛?⬛, about two-thirds of the rain ⬛?⬛ the rest finds its way back to the ⬛?⬛.
> In this way ⬛?⬛ moves around the ⬛?⬛ in the water cycle.

You can instead use Tray - a program which will remove letters, at random, from a piece of text which should be rich and short. This can be a very educational, collaborative exercise.

Overlay keyboards

An overlay (or Concept) keyboard is a flat A3 or A4 tablet which plugs into the computer. Later versions work without wires, rather like a remote control keyboard. It is an alternative to the QWERTY keyboard. Instead of letters on key tops you have symbols, pictures or even words. To use it you place a sheet of paper on the tablet surface and mark areas with symbols, pictures and words. You then use a special program to attach words to the areas on the keyboard. When the child presses an area on the tablet, words are typed into the computer.

The keyboard overlay can be a memory jogger and a great help with spelling. In this way the keyboard makes word processing accessible to younger as well as special needs children.

There are also software versions of overlay keyboards - programs such as 'Clicker' put the overlay pictures and words on the screen and dispense with a physical keyboard. The children then mouse click on these pictures and words instead of the keyboard. You may well find these software overlays easier to set up than a plug in keyboard.

Word processing ideas

Writing stories

The children can use the word processor to develop a story. For example, they can write about plants and light using the story-starter: "One day Jo woke to find the sky was dark..."

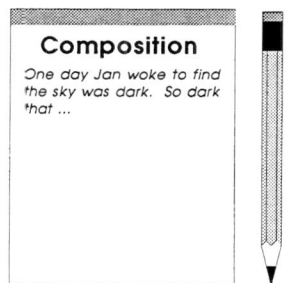

Composition

One day Jan woke to find the sky was dark. So dark that ...

Making a newspaper

A newspaper project can provide an excellent focus for science work. For example, the children might prepare a science magazine or a recycling campaign newspaper.

The newspaper might talk about the kinds of materials that can be recycled and how these materials find their way back into use. It can explain how glass can be melted and reused, and it can say why glass is sorted into different colours. It might talk about the quality of recycled paper and the uses of recycled paper. It can be illustrated.

A class science magazine can feature the discoveries of members of the class. The children can talk about the investigations they did and include pictures of themselves. They might talk about their noise survey or about an investigation to find the best brand of trainers.

There is scope here for a whole class project. You can have teams of picture editors, reporters, sub-editors, printers and so on, all working to an agreed production schedule.

You need a program that gives a decent print-out. You may also need time, but the evidence to date indicates that children benefit from such activity enormously.

World Wide Web

Computer

Phone line

Modem

The Internet - connect up to the world

The Internet opens up the possibilities for sharing this work with others, whereever they may be in the world. With a computer, a modem, a phone line and a subscription to an Internet service, such as BT CampusWorld or RM's Eduweb, children can post 'Web pages' on the Internet or start up a dialogue with others. They might post a question to a scientist or exchange ideas with other schools. It is hard to overestimate the potential here for injecting a 'live' and unpredictable element into your work.

Planning an investigation

What this is about

This is about using a word processor to plan an investigation. You use a word processor to write prompt questions, such as those below, and then save the file on disk. Then, when the children are doing a planning exercise, let them use the file as a prompt sheet.

The title of our investigation is...

We are trying to find out if ...

What I think will happen is ...

We think this will happen because ...

We will need the following to do this investigation ...

What we will do is ...

What we will measure or look for is ...

In our investigation, we will change...

In our investigation, we will keep the following things the same ...

To be safe we will make sure that ...

I have learnt that ...

IT tools

Section

2

A word about printing

Printing work from the computer is so important. You can look at your work and test how it looks or how it reads - much better when you are away from the computer. And being able to produce a quality printout can seriously change your children's aspirations: if the end-product justifies more effort they make more effort. It is such a shame that printing is the least reliable aspect of using a computer.

You may be fortunate in having a permanently set up system where you never move or change the computer, software and printer. Such machines usually have the software built-in and when you switch the machine on, it makes the necessary settings for you. Some have an intelligent plug-and-play arrangement which resolves some problems. If you have a more problematic system, here are some general 'tips' for success:

Connect up, then switch on the printer

You can damage some systems by plugging things in live, so it's safer to connect things when they are switched off.

Install the printer driver for the make of printer you use.

Your software - say, your word processor sends messages to the printer using another piece of software called a printer driver. This translates messages from the program into a code that the printer can understand. Sometimes this printer driver is part of the word processor program, but often it is a separate item. Your computer needs to have the printer driver software installed before you run other software. The hard disk on your computer can be set up to do this automatically when the machine is switched on. Otherwise, you may have to do this every time you switch on.

Check that the printer paper is in position.

If you start printing when the paper is not adjusted correctly, the margins and page breaks might be wrong.

Check the printer is set and ready. Switch it off and on if you are unsure of this.

Why? The computer expects the printer to be in its normal start-up condition when you ask it to print.

Run your software

Your word processor software may need to know what printer you are using so that it can adjust itself for the appropriate size paper, fonts or colours.

Save your work and then print your document.

It's amazing that, with the Internet, you can get your computer to talk to another miles away and yet the same machine can't talk to a printer just a metre away. Mindful of this snag, save your work before printing - if something goes wrong during printing it's rare to recover elegantly from the problem.

When you ask the computer to print, a stream of messages is sent to the printer. The first messages to be sent are the most important messages - they tell the printer what to do with later messages. That means that if you switch off the printer during printing, or the mechanism fouls up, the printer can forget what it is meant to do. The simple, but annoying remedy may be to start from scratch.

If you ask the machine to print while the printer is 'off', your computer may lock-up because it cannot send the printer any messages. Or the printout might have been stored on the disc and sit there waiting for you to rectify the problem: you will need to switch on the printer as well as tell the computer that you have done so.

Next time buy a better printer.

You can choose from several printing technologies. Whichever you choose, reliable paper transport and storage - a paper tray for example - overcomes many common printing problems. Laser printers give good black images, like a photocopier, and they are inexpensive. Ink-jet or bubble-jet printers work by squirting ink at the paper and the print quality is very good. They come in black, colour and photo versions - the photo model is the one to consider first.

Dot-matrix printers often produce grief as well as disappointing printouts. Put a 'kick-me' label on your problematic equipment - a daily kick will bring forward the day when you have to replace it with something less stress inducing. By all means persist with what you have, but a printer you can trust will reduce stress levels and change aspirations.

Graphics programs

Graphics are a child's first language. Tools which allow children to illustrate their investigations and observations can only help them to communicate better. It is hard to imagine a piece of scientific work without graphics.

Drawing programs allow children to draw perfect lines, rectangles and circles. That alone makes them valuable for drawing diagrams. They also allow children to easily correct errors, make things bigger or smaller or copy a picture from one place to another. They can build up a library of pictures and constantly recycle them. They can even use clip-art libraries - discs you can buy with lots of pictures on one topic. They might drop these pictures into stories, reports and word processor tables and save much time and effort. With a set of animal pictures on the screen you might even set-up a sorting-out exercise. There are however, programs like My World (Semerc), listed throughout the Ideas Section, which are specifically set up for this type of exercise.

For some types of illustration, photographs are essential. There are various devices to get photographs into the computer. One is the scanner - an affordable accessory which teachers and children will find many uses for. It allows you to use pictures in your work with ease. Another device is the digital camera which, as it uses magnetic disc rather than film, gives you instant photographs. This makes so many projects realistic it ought to be an essential resource. Children might use one to record their investigations or make a pictorial database of creatures they found on a field trip. But the cheapest and most accessible idea will be to get your ordinary photographs developed straight onto a CD-ROM disc, called a Photo-CD.

Science is rich in processes that need a moving image to explain them. Children might use a video camera to record minibeasts in the field action or even their investigations. There is also 'multimedia authoring' - where children use a word processor, Internet tools or special multimedia programs to assemble pictures, sounds and video. It is not hard or much different from putting a picture in a word processed page. The result is unusual however: the resulting pages allow the reader to access the information as their interests dictate, instead of working through it like a book. For some purposes - such as a project on the solar system, a multimedia project may be the ideal way of approaching the subject.

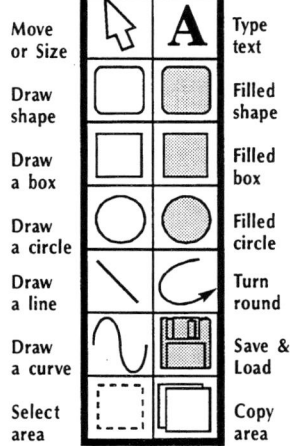

Move or Size		Type text
Draw shape		Filled shape
Draw a box		Filled box
Draw a circle		Filled circle
Draw a line		Turn round
Draw a curve		Save & Load
Select area		Copy area

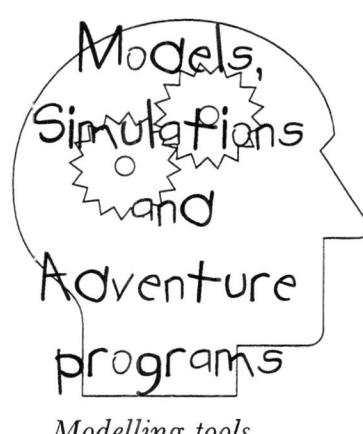

Models, Simulations and Adventure programs

Modelling tools

Modelling

The natural and physical world is complex. In science we try to understand it, or parts of it, by breaking it down into manageable parts. We build models to represent these parts.

A 'part' of the world might be the home, a forest, a seashore, or even the human body. A computer program, perhaps on a CD-ROM, or on CD-I (Philips' Compact Disc Interactive) can model these. It can give us a chance to explore, to play with variables, to test ideas and gain an insight into how things tick.

Model builders, simulation programs and adventure games are the sorts of computer programs that allow us to do this. Each is a distinct type of program although that distinction is frequently blurred in practice.

Model builders and spreadsheet programs allow you to build models, to explore and to change them. Simulation and adventure programs merely allow you to explore what they provide.

Modelling s fascinating and thought-provoking. There are many gripping science examples that are well worth exploring. Modelling can tax the brain heavily and will miss some children completely. But now and then you will find a piece of software which makes a difficult idea much more accessible. These are listed, under their respective topics, throughout the Ideas Section - look for the *IT: Modelling* labels.

IT tools

Section

2

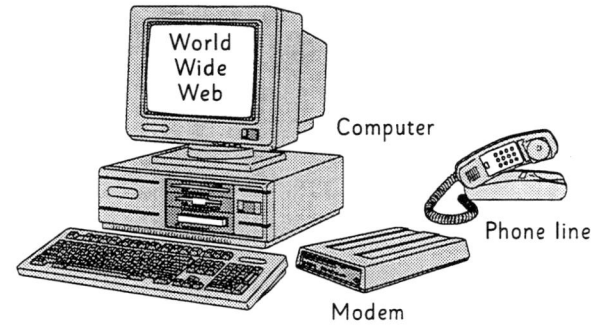

World
Wide
Web

Computer

Phone line

Modem

The Internet

There is a rumour that the Information Superhighway will be the greatest new technology. That it will change lives and education. As rumours go there is a good chance this might be true: the idea that you could get any piece of information to the classroom at the click of a button, even pictures and multimedia software is an attractive one.

While the Information Superhighway isn't here yet, we do have now is an information highway called the 'Internet' - for UK schools it's called the 'National Grid for Learning'. For a hundred pounds, you can connect a school computer to it using a phone line.

You need a modem that will turn computer signals into noises that travel along phone lines in the same way that voices do. You also need an 'online service', a firm who provides you with software and a number for your computer to call and 'connect' to.

But within a minute of dialling the phone number, you could be 'surfing' for science resources - finding out about the world use of energy, the life of polar bears or all there is to know about planet Mars.

You can turn pages of words and pictures, as you might in a book or encyclopaedia. And there are 'forms' you can fill in to search for things. You will not just be searching the books in the school library - but every book, every encyclopaedia, stored in computers all over the world. You can even visit places like museums and habitats. It is as if you had an unlimited stock of CD-ROM discs ready to explain anything you needed to. Schools are using it, not to just collect information, but to share ideas, and add their own information.

Unlike a book or CD-ROM the Internet is dynamic - there are weather reports which change by the hour. It is also unpredictable, anarchic even - there are no guarantees about what you will find - but find something you will.

The key piece of advice is to find a good start page, called a portal, where other people, acting like librarians, can save you a lifetime of searching. For starters check out the ASE - organising the Internet for schools is a huge task, but they will know someone. Also take a look at www.rogerfrost.com where you will places to go, ideas and pointers to resources for using computers and science.

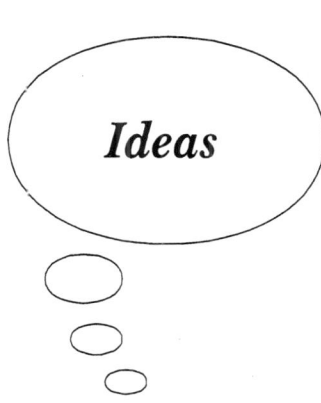

Ideas

Ideas for using information technology in science work

Using IT develops pupils' skills in handling information. These skills are not only valuable 'life skills' but they also enable them to delve deeper into science.

The ways in which information technology can help science are varied. It can help pupils to understand. It can offer a focus for discussion. It can prov de access to rich source materials. It may simply remove unnecessary effort - which on the surface saves time, but looking deeper brings pupils closer to using what we call 'higher order skills'.

This section shows the very many points in the science curriculum where IT can help teach science. I hope readers will be encouraged to build some of these ideas into their teaching and get a measure of what IT can add to science.

Key to the entries in this section:

Science 'idea' headings are...

... followed by one or more science activities

... which are described - what to do, what **software** or **hardware** to use and some questions you car ask or explore. Where appropriate, the description gives a reason why the activity is useful and what it is trying to teach.

Software titles is listed so: **Bodymapper** (Age 4-13, PC/Arc/Mac from TAG) which shows age suitability, machine version and the supplier. Addresses are given at the end.

*Then, there are the small print **footnote** entries showing which information technology skills are involved. This may be: Handling information, Communicating using IT, Measuring, Controlling or Modelling with IT.*

Recommended software

Choosing software, like choosing any book is subject to taste and teaching style. Where software has merit and been used successfully it has been recommended - the opposite is also true. I was unable to see a number of interesting titles in time for publication and have included them without recommendation or condemnation. You are especially welcome to address recommendat ons to me at the publishers. There's now a book with full reviews of the software called 'Software for Science Teaching' available through the suppliers on the cover leaf.

Using IT in... ourselves

The parts of the body

All about the body

You have a very good choice of CD-ROM software to allow children to get to know the body. Dorling Kindersley's **The Ultimate Human Body 2** (age 9-16, CD-ROM PC/Mac on mail order) is the most impressive of these and children could use the section called 'The body machine'. Younger pupils could use the section where they remove parts of the body but more appropriate is DK's **My Most Amazing Human Body** (age 6-10, CDROM PC/Mac mail order) - see the section on eating and exercise. **3D Body Adventure** (age 10-16, CD-ROM for PC on mail order) is fun, gets you wearing 3D glasses and is well worth a look. Microsoft's **Magic Bus Explores the Human Body** (Age 6+, CD-ROM for PC on mail order) is excellently produced and a great deal of fun - too much fun really. **Wonders of learning - The Human Body** (age 5-9, CD-ROM for Mac on mail order) is an uninspired picture book which reads to the children. **Understanding the Body** (age 12-16, CD-ROM for PC/Mac/Arc from Anglia) is for older children, covers the body in detail and has pictures you can use. **How your body works** (age 11+ CD-ROM on mail order/Mindscape) has excellent animation though it's more a home title.

There are other, still good, titles which do not require a CD-ROM system - **BodyWise** (age 9-14, Archimedes from Sherston) has body labels, animation, graphics and a quiz. **Bodymapper** (age 4-13, PC/Arc/Mac from TAG) is a deserving award winner with 'make your own body labels', and an 'ourselves' database. While in **Learn about the Human Body** (age 4-9, Mac from TAG) the children can take away layers of the body and see the parts labelled. **All about Ourselves** (age 4-7, PC/Mac from SEMERC) is made for school and is likely to find favour - a body labelling exercise is one of its many components.

IT: Modelling

What do the parts of the body do?

The class can do research on the organs of the body. They can agree on the type of information they want, be that what the organ does, where it's found and how big it is. They can then use a **word processor** to create a table. The word processor allows them to produce a collective effort without the usual mix of handwriting.

IT: Communicating

What types of joint can you find in the body?

Find out about the different types of bone joints in the body - use a book or a CD-ROM such as Dorling Kindersley's **Ultimate Human Body 2** (CD-ROM for PC/Mac - mail order). Record your findings in a table on your **word processor**. The word processor helps the children to work as a team and allows them to edit their writing as their ideas develop. They can list the types of joint they find, where they might find them and what kind of movement they do. **Skeleton** (Age 8-13, for DOS PC/Arc from AVP) is a unique program where children practise measuring using their body. They enter the size of their bones and can print out a life-size bone or indeed a whole skeleton. The PC version looks outdated - though it does work. Younger children can also assemble their bones, but on screen using **My World - Skeletons** (PC/Arc from Semerc). In **Learn about Skeletons** (age 4-9, Mac from TAG) the children can again construct and print out a human skeleton. Dorling Kindersley's **Ultimate Human Skeleton** (CD-ROM for PC/Mac - mail order) 'looks' good but there is much here you would not ever use.

IT: Handling information / Modelling

Using IT in... ourselves

Do you know your body?

When you have done some research work on the parts of the body you can use a **branching database program** to build up a key about them on the computer. The children have to think of a 'part' and the computer will ask

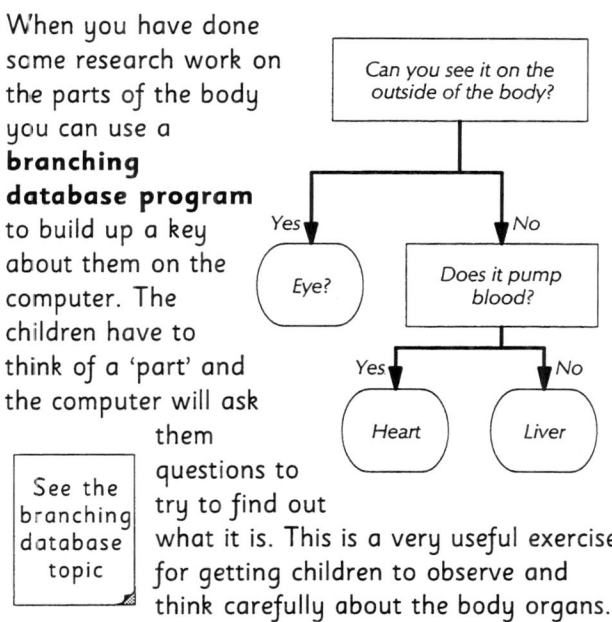

them questions to try to find out what it is. This is a very useful exercise for getting children to observe and think carefully about the body organs.

> See the branching database topic

IT: Handling information

Which muscles are the strongest?

You can compare the strength of different muscles using forcemeters and bathroom scales. You might ask the children how they could measure the strength of their thumb or their legs, triceps or biceps. Which muscles do they think are the strongest? How do their results show this? A **spreadsheet** provides a ready-made table for recording the results - it will also allow them to draw a bar graph showing their muscles' strength. What do the tallest bars tell them? Can they sort the muscles into two groups - strong muscles and weak muscles?

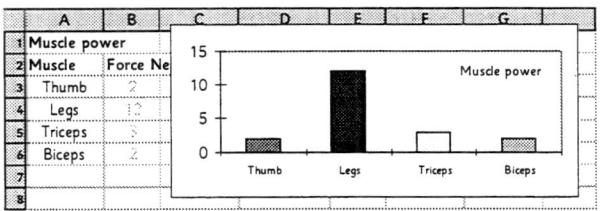

IT: Handling information

How we differ

About me

Younger and special needs children can fill in screens with information about themselves using **My World - Me** (PC/Arc from Semerc).

What is the most common eye colour?

You can do a survey of eye colours and use a **database program** to record the results. You might ask: what is the most common eye colour?

> See the database topic

Does it have anything to do with your hair colour? How would you show if it has? The children can choose from a table, a pie chart or a bar chart for the best way to display the answers to these questions.

IT: Handling information

How do we differ?

You can do a survey of children in the class and answer a range of questions on how we differ. For example, you might ask if girls are taller, or if tall people have bigger hands or if those with long legs jump higher? Does height have anything to do with shoe size? How are our  reaction times different? Is our lung capacity different? Does lung capacity have anything to do with our chest size? And so on - but see the worked example in the database section. With older pupils, this activity offers an opportunity for testing ideas, measuring and analysing data. Younger pupils should focus on just a few questions - as in the previous two activities. You can put the data into a **database program** -

> See the database topic

or with much less fuss into **Bodymapper** (age 4-13, PC/Arc/Mac from TAG) - a program which also has a lot of information about the body. It is good introduction to a database program.

IT: Handling information

Using IT in... ourselves

How high can you leap?

Similar to the previous activity, you can do a survey of how high people jump but this time use a **spreadsheet** program to record the results. The spreadsheet gives you a ready-made recording table and can produce pie charts and bar charts: which graph best shows the results of the class? Do people who can leap higher have anything in common?

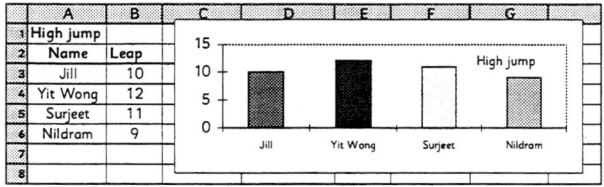

IT: Handling information

Who has the biggest hands?

Some hands are bigger than others - you might pick up as much sand as you can and then weigh the sand. What feature of your hand helps you to pick up the most sand? Is it your hand span? Your thumb size? Try this with the class - weigh the sand they can hold and measure their hands. You can record your results in a **database program** - and then draw scattergraphs of say, sand against hand span, to see if there is a pattern. What do you find? Who has the biggest hands? If someone said they had big hands, what would you measure to find out? This is an interesting project for a bright group and it involves lots of measurement and data handling.

Who has the biggest hand?				
Name	Sand	Thumb	Middle	Span
Jill				
Yit Wong				
Surjeet				
Nildram				

IT: Handling information

How we grow

How do we grow?

Our bodies do not grow uniformly - for example, the trunk grows much faster than the head. You might take a child of average height from each age group and line them up. You take measurements of head, trunk, legs, arms and overall height. You use a **database program** to record the results. Using a **spreadsheet** you could sort the list into order and plot a set of graphs - one for head, one for arms and so on. You might ask: which part of the body grows faster? Which part grows slower?

IT: Handling information

Write a diary telling how a baby grows inside its mother?

Children can draft and develop their written work using a **word processor**. They might write about the growth of a baby, and use a diary-style. They might work as a team, print it out, discuss it further and refine it.

IT: Communicating

Using IT in... health

The senses

How fast are your reactions?

You can measure reaction time using a pair of switch-type sensors - light switches, **light gates**, pressure pads and crocodile connectors that you find in sensor kits. One person breaks a light beam or jumps on  a pressure pad or bangs two pieces of metal together (using the connectors) and the other then has to break the light beam on another sensor. The software will show the reaction time. Can you get a consistent answer? Or does your reaction time improve after a few goes? Are your reactions better in the morning or in the afternoon? Do you react better to 'seeing' or 'hearing'? Can you suggest reasons for your findings?

IT: Measuring

How do the ear and eye work?

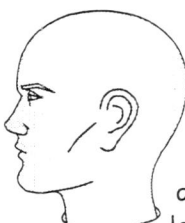 A **sound sensor** is a very good model of how the ear works. It is a microphone with a membrane that vibrates in a similar way to the ear drum. Likewise the **light sensor** is a good model of the eye: it has a lens to collect the light, a light sensitive part like the retina. Then, in both cases, there are wires (like nerves) to carry a message to the computer (or brain).

IT: Model

Which flavours are easiest to taste?

How could we show that our eyes affect our sense of taste? The children can try to identify different jelly flavours, with and without a blindfold, to see how important sight is. They might record their results in a **spreadsheet** program - and then make a bar chart. Which jelly is the easiest to identify? Do people make more mistakes when blindfolded? What clues do our eyes give us? Do you think smelling the jelly helps? Do you think smelling the jelly is more important than tasting it?

	A	B	C	D	E
1	Jelly tasters				
2	Name	Raspberry	Orange	Stawberry	Lemon
3	Jill	Yes			
4	Yit Wong	Yes			
5	Surjeet	Yes			
6	Nildram	Yes			

IT: Handling information

Exercise

Does your breathing and pulse change when you exercise?

When you exercise, your muscles need extra oxygen and sugar. Children can measure how many times they breathe in 30 seconds before, during and immediately after some exercise. What does exercise do to their breathing? How do their lungs help the muscles during exercise? Try measuring your pulse too - what does exercise do to your pulse? How does your heart help your muscles during exercise? You can record your heart sounds using a **sound sensor** pressed to your chest. Special **breathing** and **pulse sensors** can be connected to the computer too. Pulse reading wrist watches make an inexpensive alternative.

IT: Measuring

Ideas

Section

3

Using IT in... health

Who is the fittest?

How could you find out who is the fittest? Fitness has something to do with how quickly our bodies return to normal after exercise. The children can collect pulse or breathing readings from others in the class. They can record their results in a **spreadsheet** program and use these to draw graphs. How does the graph show who reached the highest pulse? Is this person the fittest? How does the graph show who is the fittest?

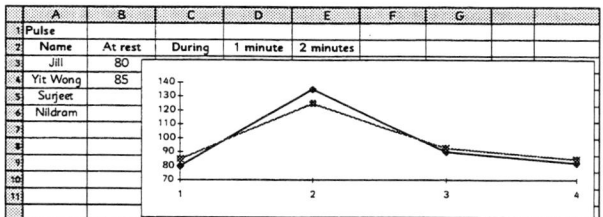

IT: Handling information

Does your temperature change when you exercise?

When you exercise you use energy and some of this appears as body heat. You can use a temperature sensor to measure this by holding a **temperature sensor** in your hand, or taping it to your body. Start the computer recording and measure your temperature as you rest, exercise and recover. Does your temperature rise when you exercise? Does it rise immediately you start to exercise? How soon does your temperature return to normal? How does the graph show you this?

IT: Measuring

Is there water in our breath?

There is a little water in the air, but we add to it when we breathe out. This water comes from our food. You can use a **humidity sensor** to measure the water level in the air you breathe. You simply breathe out over the sensor and watch the trace of the screen rise. Is there more water in the air or in the air you breathe out? If you exercise (i.e. you burn more food) do you breathe out more water? Why do you think this happens?

IT: Measuring

How do hospitals keep us alive?

See the control topic

You can use a computer **control box** to imitate a baby incubator. You might use a **temperature sensor** and a battery operated fan connected to a control box. You then write a control program to monitor the temperature and switch on the fan if the temperature goes above a certain level. This is also a very good 'model' of the way we keep our body temperatures steady. See the control section for a worked example.

IT: Control

How can we keep healthy?

You can get the children to research the ways we can keep healthy and they can use the computer to produce a poster on this. So they might cover food, exercise, drugs or smoking and include pictures with their information, statistics or whatever. The computer helps, not just in assembling the elements in the poster but in allowing them to test a draft on their audience.

IT: Communicating

What do you know about drugs?

Drug Sense tells about drugs and their effects using cartoon characters. More than facts there are plenty of exercises and games to reinforce the information. This is a rare, high quality title (age 7-11 for PC/Mac from New Media or mail order).

Why do people smoke?

To make children aware of how they can be drawn into a dangerous habit, the children can do a survey to find out why people took up smoking. They might start by discussing what they could find out by doing such a survey and move on to recording and analysing their results with a **database program**.

IT: Handling information

Using IT in... food

How much sleep do you get?

The children can do a survey to find out how much sleep people get. They might raise questions such as: do older people get less sleep, or do girls have earlier bedtimes than boys? Using these questions you choose the information you need to collect - for example, bedtimes, waking times, sex and age. You can then enter the results into a **database program** - a program which stores the data in a systematic way and allows the children to analyse their data. They might get the program to calculate the amount of sleep each person gets. Or they can draw a histogram or count graph showing how sleep varies across different age groups. And if they repeat this graph with just the girls' data and with just boys' data, they can compare the two graphs side by side - do girls have earlier bedtimes than boys?

IT: Handling information

Do people with wider chests have bigger lungs?

Larger people need more lung capacity - if only because they have more flesh to feed with air. The children might suggest that taller people have bigger lungs. They might discuss how they can measure how big their lungs are. They could try two approaches - one is to measure their chest size before and after a big breath. Another is to blow into a tube inside a large upside-down container of water - and then measure the water displaced. They can record their results, such as height, chest size and lung size in a **database program**. This they can use to draw graphs. For example, they can sort the database on children's height and then plot a bar graph of lung size. A steady increase in the bars shows that your lung size does increase with your height. How then does your lung size change with your chest size?

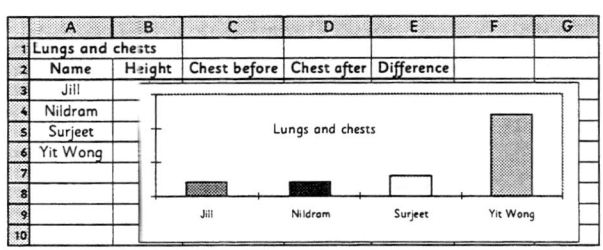

IT: Handling information

What foods will give us a good diet?

The children can research a food and use the **word processor** to produce an advertisement about it. They might cover cereals, bread, fruits, nutrients or additives and include pictures with their information. If they need to use photographs from packaging they can capture them for the computer using a hand **scanner**. The computer helps, not just in assembling the elements in the poster but in allowing them to prepare a first draft for market research.

IT: Communication

What do we mean by 'food gives us energy'?

Burning some food - a biscuit, a crisp or peanut is the classic way to illustrate that foods contain energy. You burn the food to heat up a container of water. By placing a **temperature sensor** in the water you can show the rise in temperature very graphically on the computer screen. You might ask: what does the graph 'do'? Why does it rise? Where does the energy come from? How do foods compare?

IT: Measuring

How long should we leave frozen food to thaw?

You can freeze the end of a **temperature probe** inside a sausage - and then take it out of the freezer to record the temperature as it thaws. The computer screen will show how long the food takes to thaw. Does the temperature go up steadily? Does it change all of a sudden? Why does food packaging tell us to defrost the product thoroughly before cooking? Is it possible to cook the food - in say, hot water and the inside remain cold? How could we show this?

IT: Measuring

What helps bread dough to rise?

Yeast, a live fungus, needs warmth to make bread. You can monitor the rise of bread dough by resting the lever arm of a **position sensor** on the dough. 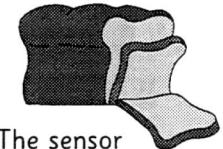 The sensor will show the rise of the dough as a graph rising up the screen. You can ask: how could we find out if the bread will rise faster in the warm? And even: will the bread rise faster if we give the yeast extra sugar?

IT: Measuring

Which cereals are the most nutritious?

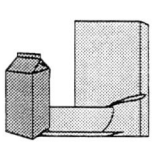 Get the children to prepare a table about cereals using a **word processor** - an exercise which involves organising data. They can use the list of ingredients on the packaging and then record whether the cereal has oats or wheat, has sugar, honey, salt, yeast, milk powder and so on. You can discuss the roles of the various ingredients - for example, honey is better than sugar, milk powder makes it creamy, salt brings out the taste. Which ingredients provide energy? Which ingredients provide fibre? Which ingredients are cosmetic?

IT: Communicating

Which is the most popular fruit?

The children can do a survey to find the most popular fruits - an exercise to get them to record, organize and analyse data. They might use a checklist and ask which fruit is liked best, or they 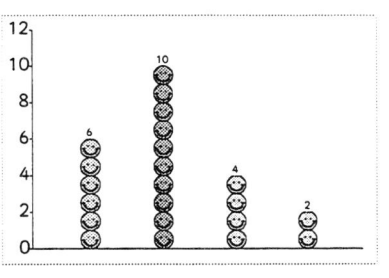 might score a list of fruits - scoring their favourite as 1, the next favourite as 2 and so on. They can place their results in a **graphing program** to produce a bar graph. What does the graph tell them? Are there other types of graph, which would show the results better?

IT: Handling information

Which foods have the most energy and fibre?

You can answer many questions using the nutrition information panels on food: which food has the most sugar? Which has the least fibre? Which has the most protein and the least sugar? The children can use their recording skills to enter nutrition information into a **database program**. And as they analyse the data they will learn about the key ingredients in food. Using the program they can sort the foods to find which has the most of each ingredient, they can search for those foods with protein more than... and sugar less than... If you restrict the foods to cereals or spreads, you'll have a set of data to make some useful comparisons. There is also the **Food Glorious Food** datafile to run with the **Pinpoint** database program (age 9-14, For PC/Arc from Logotron). **Diet Guide** (age 9-14, For Arc from Hampshire) is not just a database about food, but a great program to analyse your diet easily. This is a good program, but the male professor in the program, is a 'bad' image.

Breakfast cereals							
Cereal	Energy	Protein	Carbo	(Sugar)	Fat	Fibre	Sodium
Puffed wheat	1370	15.3	62.4	0.3	1.3	5.6	0.004
Honey Nut	1626	6.1	18.3	33.3	5.2	4.6	0.6
Chocohoops	1832	6.1	74	27.4	12.7	2.8	0.3

IT: Handling information

Using IT in... food

How much of a banana is edible?

Different size bananas provide different amounts of edible banana and you can do an interesting 'scientific analysis' exercise to practise some maths. You will need a couple of different brands of bananas and weigh the fruit before and after peeling. You enter the results into a **spreadsheet** program and use it to calculate the amount of edible fruit. You can get the program to draw a bar graph to compare the bananas: which brand has the most flesh? You could take cost into account too - and use the spreadsheet to calculate how much flesh you get for your money.

Similarly, you might compare brands of pop corn - they give different amounts of popped corn when you cook them. Here you can measure the weight of corn you use, how much gets popped and how much it costs. Using a **spreadsheet** you can prepare a *Which?* report to point to the best brand.

	A	B	C	D	E	F
1	Bananas					
2	Brand	Weight	Cost	Whole weight	Peeled weight	Cost of banana
3		g	£	g	g	£
4	Canaries					
5	M&S					

IT: Handling information

Can you design a balanced diet?

You can get the children to design a balanced diet - putting them in the role of dietician in a hospital. You tell them that each meal must have some fruit, some starchy food and some protein and then they can use the **word processor** to design a meal. They can offer their meal for discussion - and when they are happy with it, they can turn it into an attractive menu card.

IT: Communicating

Where does food come from?

When you have done some research on foods you can play a 20-questions game on foods - one person thinks of a food, while the others have to ask questions to find what it is. After this you can use a **branching database** program to build up a similar set of questions on the computer. The database will allow you to identify any food by answering a few questions. This exercise encourages children to think 'scientifically' about food.

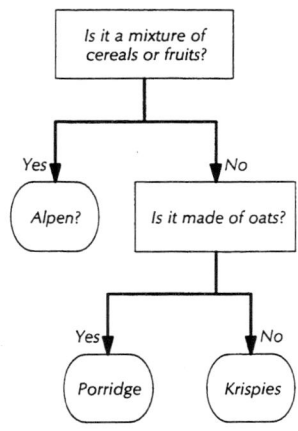

IT: Handling information

Using IT in... animals

Variation and classification

All about minibeasts

You can get the children to use a CD-ROM or database of minibeasts for a project. They might find out how an animal moves, how big it is, how many legs and how many wings it has. They can describe how many parts its body has, and how it is camouflaged. You might use **Garden Wildlife** (age 7-11, CD-ROM for PC/Mac/Arc from Anglia) which has information and photographs on over a hundred garden creatures.

It is nice, simple to use and great if you are 'into' wildlife. Older children can use the **Minibeasts database** (age 11-18, Key datafile for most computers from Anglia/AVP), where there is plenty of data, though largely text and numbers. The Key database program allows you to draw graphs to look for patterns such as "do insects have a favourite food". There are many more ideas you can explore: which creatures have eight legs? Do spiders have wings? Which creatures have two wings? Which creatures have four wings? Why do they have four wings?

Creepy Crawlies (age 9+, CD-ROM for PC/Mac/Arc on mail order) has information, pictures and text on around 70 animals. The coverage is broader than minibeasts, the video clips are too short and the commentary is distracting. The information is useful and it is easy to use - making this just OK. **Bugs - An Insect Adventure** (age 9+, CD-ROM for PC on mail order) is better, more exciting but really more for the home. **Insects** for PC from Ransom/AVP) is better still - identifying keys, insect sounds, beetle-maker and interesting bits of film - very likeable and diverse things to do. **Spiders** (age 5-9, CD-ROM for Mac from RM) is a picture book which reads the text to the children. It's acceptable. Another title in the same series is **Butterflies** (age 6-8, CD-ROM for PC/Mac from RM) - a glossy picture book would be as good. **Butterflies of the World** (age 11-adult, CD-ROM for PC/Mac on mail order) is for fans only.

Younger and special needs children can assemble minibeasts, build minibeast scenes and show life cycles and food webs using the lovely **My World**

2 - More minibeasts (PC/Arc from Semerc).

Learn about Insects (age 4-9, Mac from TAG) is worth a look.

All about dinosaurs

There are several CD-ROM titles with all you want to know about dinosaurs. They get the children thinking about the diversity of life: which dinosaurs had tails? How did they protect themselves? What did they eat? Which ones would make a meal of you?

Many CD-ROMs are aimed at a higher level but most have picture you can use in projects.

Microsoft's **Dinosaurs** (age 10+, CD-ROM for PC/Mac - mail order) is exciting enough to be worth having - and even though the videos are poor. Dorling Kindersley's **Dinosaur Hunter** (age 9+, CD-ROM for PC/Mac - mail order) is worth having in a library - it's designed more for browsing than finding things. Another above average title, also produced for the home market, is **3D Dinosaur Adventure** (age 8+, CD-ROM for PC/Mac - mail order). This allows you to see dinosaurs from different angles, watch dinosaur movies and read about them. **Dinosaurs** (age 5-9, CD-ROM for Mac from RM) is simply a picture book where the text is read - it's for the young or special needs. **Dinosaurs Multimedia Encyclopaedia** (age 10+, CD-ROM for PC/Mac - mail order) is less than average. **Prehistoria** (age 9+, CD-ROM for Mac on mail order) is broader than dinosaurs and would support history work too. It has poor video but good pictures, readable text and speech. There is also a **Dinosaurs datafile** to run with the **Pinpoint** database program (age 9-13, For PC/Arc from Logotron) - but it's not as much fun as CD-ROM.

Younger and special needs children can assemble dinosaurs, fit them in landscapes and do simple matching activities using **My World 2 - Dinosaurs** (PC/Arc from Semerc). **Learn about Dinosaurs** (age 4-9, Mac from TAG) is worth a look.

IT: Handling information

Ideas

Section

3

Using IT in... animals

Can you identify an animal?

Getting the children to build a **branching database** on animals is an excellent way to make them observe animals closely. You can start with a collection of animal pictures and sort them into groups. Or you can play a '20 questions' game where the class have to guess the

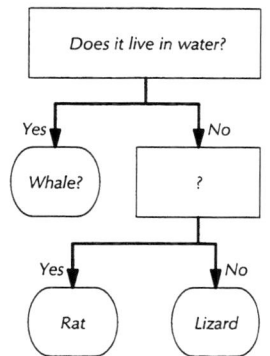

See the branching database topic

animal one child has chosen. After these starter activities they use the branching database program to 'teach' the computer about the animals in their collection.

IT: Handling information

What are our favourite pets?

The children can do a survey to find the most popular pets - an exercise in recording and organising data. They might give out a list and ask their peers which pet they like best, or they might get them to score their favourite as 1, the next favourite as 2 and so on. They can put the results into a **graphing program** and produce a pie chart. What does the graph tell them? Is the winning pet way ahead of the second best? Are the less popular pets much less popular?

Children can add ready-made pictures of zoo animals, birds and pond life to their written work with **Just Pictures** (PC/Arc/Mac from Semerc).

IT: Handling information

Can you make a device to feed the cat?

Using a computer **control box** you can create a device which meters out food during the day. The children can use a control program to activate the device at certain times of the day.

IT: Control

What is alive?

The children can do a survey of a patch of ground, and list and sort out the things they find. They might use a portable computer to take notes, but whatever, they can use a **word processor** to sort the things they find into living, non-living, once living but now dead or never living. Modern word processors make it very easy to move text around on screen to experiment with their ideas.

IT: Handling information

How do animals keep warm?

You might have heard that penguins huddle together to keep warm. This shows how animals adapt to their environment. The children can investigate whether this really helps them - by using tins of hot water dressed as furry mammals. They could arrange one tin on its own, and another as part of a huddle. They

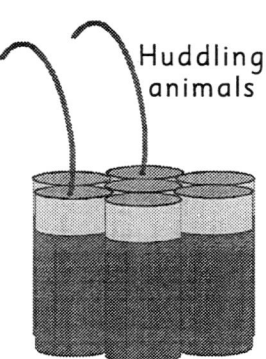

could then use **temperature sensors** to compare how fast the lone and the huddling animals cool. This activity requires some good planning and it's worth doing a test run and discussing ways to make it fair.

You can also see how fur helps animals in their environment - investigating any of these questions using tin cans, warm water and **temperature sensors**: how does fur help an animal? Does fur still work when it is wet? When animals are cold, skin muscles pull their hair up straight - does 'fur up' work better than 'fur down'?

IT: Measuring

Using IT in... animals

How do animals keep cool?

The elephant's ears work like a heat radiator - allowing them to keep cooler in hot conditions. The children can make elephant ears out of cooking foil and then attach them to a tin. You can fill  the tin with hand-hot water and they can measure how fast the water cools using sensors. If you have two **temperature sensors** you can compare this with a tin 'without ears'. A desk fan will help speed the cooling. Have they made the investigation a fair test? What does the graph on the screen tell them?

IT: Measuring

How does our pet live and grow?

Having a pet is a good opportunity to study and record how it lives and grows. The children can record how the pet behaves and how fast it grows. They can weigh it daily or measure how much it drinks and eats. They can keep their observations in a **word processor** - adding bits daily. Unlike a paper diary it need never be spoiled by a messy entry. Daily measurements can be kept in a **spreadsheet** program - building up day by day to show the pet's growth. Is there a growth spurt? Is there a pattern in the results? Does the pet eat more as it gets bigger?

A	B	C	D	E	F
Basil's weight chart					
Date	Weight				

If you place a **light sensor** in the cage you will see a response on the screen each time the animal moves near it. So by using computer sensors you can also record the activity of a mammal over 24 hours. It will help answer questions such as, how much time is spent in the nest and whether the animal is busy by day or by night. Teachers have used all sorts of sensors to monitor animal behaviour, like putting a **temperature sensor** in a nest or putting a light sensor near a hamster's exercise wheel. In one example, a light sensor was placed, using Blutack, against a fish tank to pick up the fish's swimming movements. They covered part of the tank with black sugar paper and could record which part of the tank was the most used.

IT: Measuring

Do animals have special needs?

Suppose you were made head keeper in a safari park. What animal will you keep? What does it eat? What else do you need to provide for your animal? Does your animal prefer dark or light? Why might it like the dark? The task is a good stimulus for research on animals and their needs. To do research they can use books or CD-ROM resources (see below). Get the children to use the **word processor** to prepare an information card about each animal they keep. They can use the ready-made pictures of zoo animals in **Just Pictures** (PC/Arc/Mac from Semerc).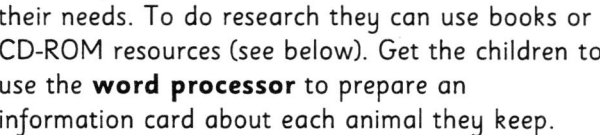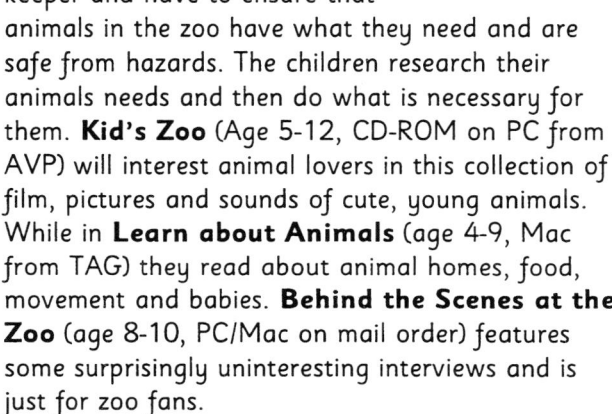
The program **ZooKeeper** (age 5-10, PC/Mac from TAG) is quite sweet and has information on 50 animals. Children again play zoo-keeper and have to ensure that animals in the zoo have what they need and are safe from hazards. The children research their animals needs and then do what is necessary for them. **Kid's Zoo** (Age 5-12, CD-ROM on PC from AVP) will interest animal lovers in this collection of film, pictures and sounds of cute, young animals. While in **Learn about Animals** (age 4-9, Mac from TAG) they read about animal homes, food, movement and babies. **Behind the Scenes at the Zoo** (age 8-10, PC/Mac on mail order) features some surprisingly uninteresting interviews and is just for zoo fans.

IT: Handling information / Modelling

Using IT in... animals

All about animals

Find out about...

The CD-ROM and the **Internet** are valuable tools for children's research on animals. They can browse out of interest and your teaching will raise questions which these encyclopaedic resources may help to answer. For example: how does the animal protect itself? How does it feed? Which animals are carnivores? Which are herbivores? Which are omnivores? How are their teeth the same?

The children can use the **word processor** to record information. They can use it to build up a table from their search or add pictures 'clipped' from the screen.

The New Dictionary / Encyclopaedia of the Living World (age 11-adult, CD-ROM Mac / PC from TAG) replaces the weaker Dictionary of the Living World (CD-ROM for Arc from TAG). It has photos, videos and the sounds of many creatures. There are distribution maps, famous biologists and the complete text of Darwin's 'Origin of Species' but it's difficult and technical. **Exploring Nature** (age 8-12, CD-ROM for PC/Arc from Hampshire) is a well above average 'field trip' where children visit different habitats, see flora and fauna and look things up in the built-in reference books. You are even given a kit (with sensors, maps, guide book and so on) to explore with - recommended though the price is high.

Microsoft's **Dangerous Creatures** (age 9-16, CD-ROM for PC/Mac from TAG) looks at 250 wild animals and has video, photos. This is good even if the text is difficult. It covers useful themes like teeth and eyes and you can re-use the material in your word processor. A primary resource pack is also available for this. Microsoft's **Explorapedia World of Nature** (age 6-10, CD-ROM for PC/Mac on mail order) is more playful, but still surprisingly good for home or library.

Animal safari (for age 9+ CD-Rom Mac/PC - Marshall Cavendish) is a look at animal life with pictures and film. It stands-up well beside Explorapedia, so do see this too.

Mammals of Africa (age 12-adult, CD-ROM for PC/Mac from mail order) is nicely put together, has information on food, skeleton and distribution - but

is quite hard; better for middle schools.

Mammals (Age 10+, CD-ROM for PC - mail order) has a nice animal identification game but it looks dated. **A World of Animals** (age 5-7, CD-ROM for Mac on mail order) just has pictures and text on whales, spiders, farm life and creatures which are popular with this age group. **World of Reptiles** (age 11+, CD-ROM for Mac from Mail order) has masses of detail - but is for reptile fans only. Dorling Kindersley's **Bird** or **Cat** (age 10+, CD-ROM for PC/Mac) are more exciting, but hard overall.

Cute and Cuddlies (age 5-7, CD-ROM for PC/Mac on mail order) covers a mixed bunch of furry animals. It shows pictures, short movies and reads to you. **Farm animals** (age 5-7, CD-ROM for Mac from RM) is a picture book and again the text is read to you. Not exciting, but maybe useful. **Farm** (age 3-8, CD-ROM for PC from New Vision) has cartoons of many farm locations and, despite appearances, will be too hard for pre-schoolers. Keen and older children can use the Key database to look for patterns in data on **Mammals of Great Britain** or **Mammals of the World** (Age 10+, Key datafiles for Nimbus/BBC/PC/Arc from Anglia/AVP). There is also an **Animal Kingdom** datafile to run with the **Pinpoint** database program (for PC/Arc from Logotron). These datafiles look dull alongside the CD-ROM resources.

IT: Handling information

Life cycles

Children can demonstrate their understanding of the life cycles of the ant, bee, ladybird, butterfly and spider using **My World 2 - Life cycles** (PC/Arc from Semerc). They have to assemble a life cycle on the screen using the pictures that come with the program. The program adds a little colour to doing the same as a paper cut-out.

IT: Modelling

Using IT in... animals

All about life in water

Pondlife (age 8-15, for BBC/Nimbus/Arc from Anglia/AVP) helps you to identify pond creatures and even shows what happens when a pond is polluted. The program idea is very good although it is let down by the limitations of these older computers. See also Seashore Life in the next section.

Microsoft's **Magic Bus Explores the Ocean** (CD-ROM PC on mail order) is a  great deal of fun and excellently produced title based around the TV series and book. The learning is very slow-going but this brightens up the topic.

Children using a **word processor** might appreciate having the ready-made pictures of pond life with **Just Pictures** (PC/Arc/Mac from Semerc).

Undersea Adventure (age 9-15, CD-ROM for PC/Mac on mail order) is an attractive encyclopaedia of the oceans - very nice reference material. **Journey with Sharks** has good movies and although it is for the home should satisfy interest while **In the Company of Whales** (age 10-adult, CD-ROM for PC from Koch Media) is from the same people yet just a bit dull. **Oceans Below** (CD-ROM for PC/Mac on mail order) is a 'virtual diving experience' where you can learn about sea life, feed an eel and your curiosity. Keen and older children can use the Key database to look for patterns in data on **Seafish** and **Freshwater Fish** (Key datafiles for Nimbus/BBC/PC/Arc from Anglia/AVP) but again these look dull alongside the CD-ROM resources.

IT: Handling information

All about habitats

The CD-ROM is a valuable tool for children's research. In **Garden Wildlife** (age 7-11, CD-ROM for PC/Mac/Arc from Anglia) you click on different habitats - tree, pond, path and lawn and see the creatures that live there. Well above average: fairly easy, spoken text, film and photographs. A identification key called 'animal expert' helps you to identify creatures. **Seashore Life** (Age 7-11, CD-ROM for PC/Mac/Arc from Anglia) has pictures and film of flora and fauna of British beaches - quite good.
Exploring Nature (age 8-12, CD-ROM for PC/Arc from Hampshire) allows children to take a field trip with a notepad, measuring instruments and information book. This is well above average but the weak teaching materials mean you'll have to work on it first. In **Being a Scientist** (age up to 11 years, CD-Rom for Mac/PC/Acorn - Anglia, £40). a woodland is the setting where children conduct experiments to find out why the trees are vanishing. Sadly the result is facile.

Picturebase - UK habitats (age 11-16, PC/Arc from AVP) is a straightforward library of pictures and spoken text about the range of habitats found here. Useful if unexciting. A **Picturebase - World habitats** disc is also available and includes desert, savannah and rain forest. **Ecodisc** (age 11-16, CD-ROM for Mac from ESM or mail order) is a good conservation modelling exercise with pictures, experts-on-hand and more. This can be recommended to middle schools. **Rainforest** (age 10+, CD-ROM for Mac on mail order) looks at geographical issues around the rain forests as well as its animals and plants - quite pretty and not bad. **A field trip to the Rainforest** (age 9+, CD-ROM for Mac from TAG) lets you explore the rain forest, see drawings of the animals and plant life and read further. **Badger Trails** (Age 9-11, for Archimedes from TAG or AVP) is a good adventure game where the children play the 'part' of a badger and try to return it to its sett. **Guardians of Greenwood** (age 9-14, CD-ROm for Acorn) described as an eco-adventure will be worth a look.

IT: Handling information

Do a habitat survey

You can do a habitat survey or minibeast safari in the park or pond to record how things live. There are many questions to ask: what animals did you see? What were they doing? Where did you see them? How many of each animal did you see? How do things change from place to place? Why might this be? How are the creatures adapted to living here? How do the animals feed? How do they move? How are the animals camouflaged? Why are they camouflaged? What do the living things here need? What do they get by living here? What happens in the winter? How did these animals get here? Which animals live in only one sort of place, which are more adaptable? Choose two animals, how are they similar? How are they different?

You will find lots to write about, lots to record and a **word processor** can help children to organize their findings. Some groups including younger groups will appreciate a computer word bank - for this you can use an overlay (**'Concept') keyboard** with your word processor. When the children need a particular word, they press on the overlay keyboard to  have it typed into their work. You have to prepare this in advance - you put pictures and useful words on a sheet on the keyboard and type the words into the program. Several suppliers (Semerc, Cleveland, Cd computing) sell packs of ready-made overlay sheets for all sorts of topics.

The children might use a **graphing program** to record how many of each sort of animal were found under a tree, in the open, under a hedge. They can also use My World 2 - More minibeasts (PC/Arc from Semerc) to assemble minibeasts, build minibeast scenes and show life cycles and food chains graphically. You might even prepare a **Concept keyboard** overlay with a map of the area drawn on an overlay - such that when they press on the map, the screen shows what was found there. Programs such as **Phases / Touch Explorer Plus** do this.

IT: Handling information

Food chains

Wot eats wot?

The children can use the **Internet** or a CD-ROM on animals to look for elusive information. Dorling Kindersley's **Eyewitness Encyclopaedia of Nature** (CD-ROM for PC/Mac on mail order), for example can be used by older children to find out about habitats and food chains. It's not comprehensive in the encyclopaedia sense of the word - and you may not find what caterpillars live on, and what eats caterpillars and what eat these - but you will find other food chains. When the children use these information sources, you might give them a focus, such as these questions: what does the animal eat? How does it eat it? Where does it get its food from? Which animals eat the same sort of food? How is the animal adapted to the food it eats? How do the beaks of seed eating birds and birds of prey compare? How do beak shapes help birds to get their food. How do the teeth of the big and small cats compare? The children 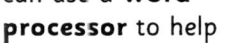 can use a **word processor** to help them record their finding in a table. They can use a **drawing program** to create a food chain on screen.

IT: Handling information

Birds

All about birds

You can get databases on disc, on CD-ROM or the **Internet** with everything you need to know about birds. While older children can use the detailed **Birds of Britain** database (Key file for most computers from Anglia) it is largely text and numbers. Given a simple choice the CD-ROM is far more attractive. **British Birds** (age 9+, CD-ROM for Acorn from The British Library) lists 250 birds, with information about habitats together with photographs and bird song. It is a fair choice. Dorling Kindersley's **Bird** (age 10+, CD-ROM for PC/ Mac) is more exciting, but hard overall. **Woodland Birds** (Age 9+, CD-ROM for Archimedes) is a look at birds and the sounds they make. The material can be used in your **word processor** but this disc is strictly for fans. **Birds and How they Grow** (age 6-10, CD-ROM for PC/Mac from RM) is an unusually easy read with information and pictures.

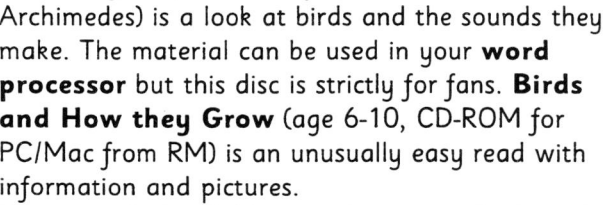

You can ask the children to choose two birds and describe their colouring and the shape of their bodies, beak, feet and legs. They can record whether they live on the ground or in trees. They can say how the two birds differ and use a **word processor** to collect their findings in a table. Some children will be able to use their 'copying and pasting' skills to take information from the ready-made pictures of birds in **Just Pictures** (PC/Arc/ Mac from Semerc).

IT: Communicating

Can you identify a bird?

A **branching database** program allows you to create a 'key' to identify birds. Give the children a set of pictures and let them use them to build up a key on the computer. See the section on branching databases for details of how to run this excellent activity.

IT: Handling information

When do birds like their lunch?

You can get the children to watch birds at a bird table - an exercise in recording and analysing data. They can use a kitchen timer to remind them to check the bird table every 30 minutes. They might record how many sparrows are at the table and then use a **spreadsheet** to store the data. Later they can draw a bar graph of the bird activity during the day: what times of day do birds like to feed. You may be able to note that sparrows feed first thing in the morning, then at lunch and then towards the end of the day.

IT: Handling information

Do birds have a favourite colour?

Computer sensors allow children to record events at a bird table automatically instead of having to check it all through the day. For example, you can attach a bag of red-dyed nuts to a spring and a **position sensor** and record how many times it moved during the day. The next day you might try again but with green-dyed nuts. The computer screen will show a series of blips and the children can be asked to use this to get a measure of how many birds have visited.

IT: Measuring

Plants

Where do flowers grow?

You can get the children to survey a green area - trying to break it up into places where different types of plant grow. You might ask: where do flowers grow? Is there anywhere plants do not grow? Are there places that plants cannot survive or take root? Can they get water here? Or light? Are they warm enough to grow? How are their seeds spread? Whatever your focus, you will find lots to write about, lots to record and a **word processor** can help children to organize this as text or as a table. They can work in groups, with different groups collaborating and developing a report on say, 'Our open space'.

Garden Planner (BBC from AVP) is a computer 'model' which lets you choose the plants for your garden and you can see it at different times of the year. It runs on older machines, so has its limitations. However, if you want something for a modern machine, you will find impressive gardening software in the shops.

Younger and special needs children can design their gardens on the screen using **My World 2 - Garden** (for PC/Arc from Semerc).

IT: Communicating / Modelling

The parts of a flower

The children can assemble the parts of a flower and look at leaf shapes using the very sweet **My World 2 - Plant Biology** (PC/Arc from Semerc). **Wild Flowers** (BBC from AVP) helps you to identify flowers by asking a series of questions. It gets children looking at the shapes of leaves and petals as they compare their flower with the graphic on the screen.

What do plants need to live?

Children can grow plants to find the conditions under which they thrive. You might ask them to plan an investigation on one of the following:

See the spreadsheet topic

would a plant grow better with fertiliser? Would a plant grow better on a slope? Can you give a plant too much water?

They can set up plants, looking at one condition each, and they can record the plants' progress in a **spreadsheet**. The program provides them with a ready-made recording grid and allows them to draw a bar graph with their results. They can look at the graph and see what difference water or fertiliser or light makes to the health of a plant.

There is a really nice program called **Botanical Gardens** (for Mac from TAG) which allows children to change the growing conditions for a plant and see the results instantly. Using this, they can fairly quickly get the idea of changing one condition at a time as well as interpreting graphs. Another good title is **PlantWise** (age 9-14, Archimedes from Sherston) which has all and more than you need to know about plants - classification, experiments, animation and nice graphics. Another title is **Learn about Plants** (ages 4-9, Mac from TAG) but the children merely read about what plants need to grow and how animals and plants work together.

IT: Modelling / IT: Handling information

Ideas

Section

3

Using IT in... plants

Are some soils warmer than others?

Different soils can hold heat better than others and this affects the growth of plants. You put trays with sand and soil under a desk lamp. You then use **temperature sensors** to measure the temperatures showing this as a graph on screen. Later you can remove the lamp and ask: Which soil heats up faster? Which soil cools down faster? How could this be important to plants?

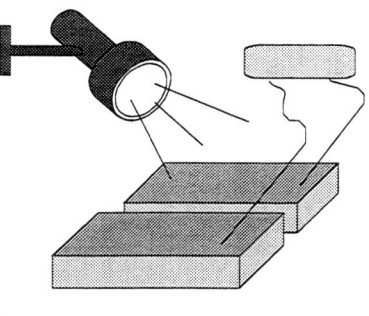

IT: Measuring

Do seeds have energy?

Growing seeds give out heat and if you put beans on wet cotton wool in a vacuum flask you will be able to measure a temperature change as they grow. You can place a **temperature sensor** in the flask and the computer will record the temperature over a day or so. You can look at the graph on the screen and ask: is there a change in temperature? Where does the heat come from? Do you think other seeds release energy? Why do you think animals eat seeds?

IT: Measuring

What would happen if the sun went out?

The children can use a **word processor** to write a story about the importance of the sun. They write about how cold it would get, or tell how plants would die and how animals depend upon plants for food.

IT: Communicating

How are fruits different?

You can give the children some picture books or a bowl of fruit and ask them to describe each fruit. They can work together at a **word processor** and develop their descriptions. Using an overlay (**Concept**) **keyboard** you can provide them with a computer word bank - such that, when they press on the overlay, words are typed into their work. You can also get the children to create a **database** of fruits and develop their skills of recording and analysing information. They can answer questions such as: do all fruits have pips? What is the most common colour of fruits? Which fruits have furry skin? Which fruits have a stone?

IT: Handling information

Do plants give off water?

Plants lose water from their leaves (transpiration) and this is how they draw nutrients from the soil. Using a **humidity sensor** you can monitor this happening - you place plant in a polythene bag and use the sensor to measure the humidity around it.

IT: Measuring

How different are leaves from the same tree?

Leaves from the same tree can be a range of sizes. The children collect 30 leaves from a single tree and measure their length, width or number of prickles or lobes. A computer **database** or **spreadsheet** program can help them to record and analyse their findings. They might draw a count graph and answer: is there a 'usual' size for a leaf? Are other leaves larger or are they smaller? Older children can look for patterns in the data. They might draw a scattergraph of holly leaf length against the number of prickles asking: do larger leaves have more prickles?

The best size for a leaf			
Leaf number	Leaf width	Leaf length	Prickles
1			
2			
3			

IT: Handling information

Using IT in... recycling

How are seeds dispersed?

The 'wings' from a Sycamore tree vary in size and fall -differently - very useful in dispersing the seeds more widely. The children can collect 30 wings and measure their length, width and how long they take to fall. A **database program** can help them to record and analyse their findings. For example, using a count graph, they can show how much the wings vary in size. Older children can take things further, they can plot a scattergraph to answer: do the wider wings fall more slowly? Do the longer wings fall more quickly?

You can do a similar exercise comparing conkers and how well they bounce. The children enter their measurements of conkers into a **database program** and try to answer: do larger conkers bounce higher or do heavier conkers bounce higher?

	A	B	C	D
1	Testing sycamore keys			
2	Key	Fall time	Length	Width
3	A			
4	B			

IT: Handling information

Can you identify this... ?

You can use a **branching database** program to create a 'key' to help you identify almost any plant. The exercise is also a good way of sharpening children's observation skills too. You collect a set of pictures of plants - or fruit, seeds, beans, leaves and the children use them to build up a key on the computer. The section on branching databases has further details of this worthy activity.

IT: Handling information

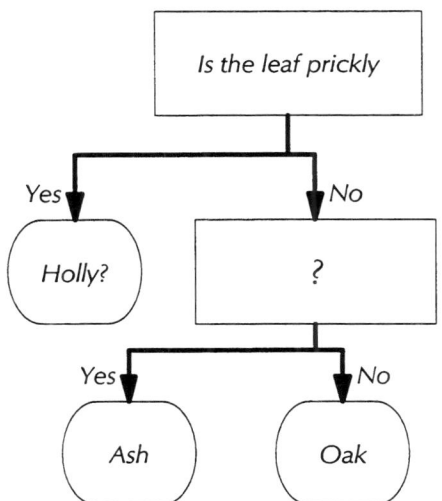

Decay

What is waste?

As an exercise on waste, children can survey the bins around the school. They can sort the waste and record what they find using a **word processor**. You might set up the word processor with a blank table and the children can fill what they find. They can say whether the item will go rusty, go mouldy, go squashy, go soggy or stay the same.

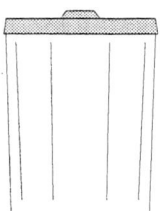

With older children you might use a more analytical tack: the children can count or weigh what they find and record this in a **spreadsheet** program. They can use the program to draw a pie chart showing the contents of a bin. You might ask: How much of our waste can be recycled? How much could be used for compost? How much will cause a problem in the future?

	A	B	C	D	E	F	G
1	Waste survey						
2	Material	Weight					
3	Paper	30					
4	Dust	1					
5	Glass	10					
6	Metal	10					
7	Vegetable	30					
8	Plastic	8					
9							

Legend: Paper, Dust, Glass, Metal, Vegetable, Plastic

IT: Handling information

Ideas

Section

3

Using IT in... materials

Human plunder

How do humans affect animals?

The children can use a **word processor** to write a newspaper article. They will need to research what it is like to be an animal displaced by the clearing of a forest or the building of a motorway. They can work as a team to draft and develop their story. They might use a hand scanner to add photographs to the piece.

The Big Green Disc (age 10-adult, CD-ROM for PC/Mac from mail order) is an attractive documentary on environmental issues. There are glorious photographs and useful data but it's more the coffee table book. **Sammy's Science House** (age 4-7, for Mac from Resource) is for the early years. It looks at weather, the environment, sequencing and classification.

Can school help with recycling?

The children can take a leading role in the school's anti-pollution or recycling campaign by using their **word processor** to create leaflets, posters and newsletters. They can raise the case for recycling glass and paper or they can write about the 'issues' such as acid rain, rainforest destruction and air pollution. They can talk about why it's important to sort glass into colours, or explain how to distinguish an aluminium can from a steel one.

Grouping materials

Which building materials are the strongest?

The children can test materials to see how strong they are and whether they would make a good building material. They might test brick, wood, iron and aluminium and see how easy they are to break or scratch. They can record their results in a **word processor** table - it allows different people to add to the table and still produce a tidy record.

There are other aspects of materials they can consider and record: they might record their colour, whether they are hard or soft, smooth or rough, wet-able or waterproof, magnetic or not, shiny or dull and conduct electricity or not. Again, all of these simple recording exercises are easily done in a word processor.

IT: Handling information

Which plastic is the most bendy?

For an interesting investigation the children can test different plastics to find which will bend the most. They will need to think about how to make their test fair - for example, it's not easy to find equal size pieces of different plastics. They will need to think about how they will measure and record their results.

A **spreadsheet** is used to record the results - the children use it to draw a bar graph. You might ask: what does the graph tell you about the plastics you tested? Does it help you sort the plastics into bendy and not bendy?

	A	B	C	D
1	How much the plastic bends			
2	Plastic	1 weight	2 weights	3 weights
3	Polythene			
4	Perspex			

IT: Handling information

Ideas

Section

3

Using IT in... materials

Can you identify this material?

You can use a **branching database** program to create a 'key' to help you identify almost any material. The exercise is a good way of sharpening children's observation skills. You collect a set of materials and the children use them to build up a key on the computer. The section on branching databases has further details of this absorbing activity.

IT: Handling information

Which material would make the best gloves for an Arctic explorer?

Children can test different materials to see which keep the heat in best. They get cups of warm water, wrap them in different materials and monitor the temperature using **temperature sensors**. Is one material as good as the next? Which material works best? What sorts of material ought to work best?

IT: Measuring

Which material is best for mopping up a spill?

How could we test fabrics to find the best one for mopping spills? How could we measure how much liquid the fabric soaks up? How can we make a fair test of this? The children might cut the different fabrics to the same size and weigh them before and after mopping up the same amount of water.

They can type their results into a **spreadsheet** and if you set this up for them, the spreadsheet will do the maths - it will work out the amount of water soaked up. They can sort the table or draw a bar graph to compare the different materials.

	A	B	C	D
1	Which is best to soak up water?			
2	Material	Dry weight	Wet weight	Amount of water
3	J cloth			
4	Nylon			
5	Newspaper			
6	Tissue			

IT: Handling information

What is it made from?

Get the children to make a list of objects and for each one suggest a suitable material to make it from. They can use a **word processor** to set the information in a table - it gives them the ability to work together. You might get them to add a column to the table with their reason why you this is the best material to use.

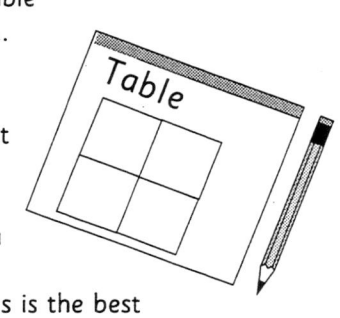

IT: Communicating

How can we identify everyday chemicals?

To build their familiarity with the behaviour of chemicals you can give the children some to test. You might set out dishes with baking powder, talc, flour, salt, sugar and cream of tartare and then ask if they could tell you what they were if the labels were lost. They can then see how they look and behave: if they dissolve in water, if they fizz in vinegar and whether they have large or small crystals. They can pool their efforts and record their findings in a **word processor** table.

To take this further, they can use a **branching database** program to make a key to identify these chemicals. This simple exercise encourages children to think 'scientifically' about the special identifying features of these chemicals. See the Branching database section for details.

IT: Communication / IT: Handling information

Which container holds the most liquid?

An important skill in 'chemistry' is the measurement of volume. The children take a set of containers and try to guess which might hold the most water. They then test their predictions and use a **graphing program** to record and display their results.

IT: Handling information

How do we test acids?

We use Universal indicator paper to test for acids and alkalis. The paper turns to one of the colours of the rainbow showing how acid something is. A group can make a poster showing the colour changes by using a **drawing program**. They can even make it into a wall chart for future reference.

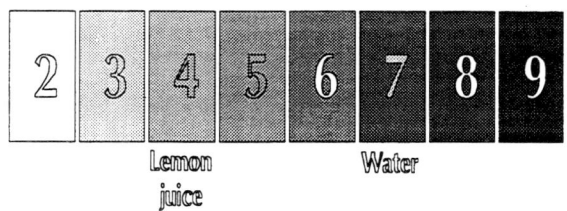

IT: Communicating

Comparing everyday things

To get children thinking about the properties that help us tell materials apart, ask them to do a 'Which' report of different soaps or different metals. For the soaps they could compare colour, smell, creaminess and texture. For the metals they could compare shine, colour, bendiness and how they scratch. For their report they can use a **word processor** - they can say what they did or they can produce a table of their results. Ask them to write a sentence about each of the things they tested.

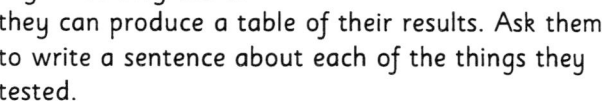

IT: Handling information

Why are things made of that?

To encourage some thought and discussion on materials, put a list of objects such as clothes, tools, toys, furniture, floor coverings and so on into a **word processor**. Ask the children to write what they have in common. For example, the materials we use for clothes are soft, warm, flexible and made of fibres.

IT: Communication

Solid, liquid or gas?

Introduce children to classifying by getting them to say if things in the room are solid, liquid or gas. They can record their thoughts in a **word processor** table: one column for the material and one for which group it belongs to. Which materials aren't they so sure about? What would a scientist say about these?

You can create a **word processor** table with three headings: solid, liquid and gas. The children have to match ideas like runny, solid, crunchy, lumpy and pours to their proper place in your table.

IT: Communicating

Using IT in... changing materials

Changing materials

Why do they put salt and sand on the roads in winter?

The children can investigate the effect of salt and sand on the melting of ice. You might pose the questions: what makes the ice melt? Does salt melt the ice or does sand melt the ice? One way to find out is to get two cups of crushed ice, sprinkle one with salt and the other with sand. You then place a **temperature sensor** in each cup to see how the temperature changes over time. Does the ice melt faster in one than the other? Is there any difference in temperature between the two cups?

IT: Measuring

Do some ice lollies freeze faster than others?

Some liquids freeze sooner than others so you can test different liquids - oil, milk, fruit juice, salty water and plain water to see how fast they freeze. You can pour some of the liquid in an ice cube tray, place this in the freezer and use a **temperature sensor** to track how fast they cool. Ask the children if they can see how the temperature graph shows that the liquid has frozen. Do the graphs help them to compare different liquids? You should find that sugary and salty liquids take longer to freeze than plain water.

IT: Measuring

What happens when we heat things?

To show how things change with heat, and practise children's observation skills, ask then to heat various items. They can put butter, an ice lolly, clay, pastry and chocolate in polythene bags and lower them into warm water. They can write about their observations and pool their ideas by using a **word processor**. Some pupils will appreciate the help of an **overlay (Concept) keyboard** which has been set up with a word bank of useful descriptors.

IT: Communicating

Which jar lets the candle burn for longer?

Large jars hold more air such that a candle will burn for longer. The children can test different size jars and record how long a candle burns for in each. They can put their results in a **spreadsheet** and use it to draw a bar graph. What does the graph tell them about the different size jars? Why could this be?

	A	B	C	D	E
1	How long will the candle stay alight?				
2	Volume cm^3	1st go	2nd go	3rd go	Avera
3	100	2	2	2	2
4	150				
5	250				
6	400		From MEU Cymru		

IT: Handling information

How does food change when we cook it?

When we cook food we change the chemicals inside it to make it more pleasant to eat or more easy to digest. Get the children to think about the foods we eat and list them in a **word processor**. Next to each food, ask them to record whether we eat the food raw and whether we eat it cooked. What does cooking do to food? Does it make it taste better? Go softer? Go runny? Smell different? Get them to add their ideas to the list.

IT: Communicating

Using IT in... changing materials

How hot does plaster get when you mix it with water?

When plaster of Paris is mixed with water, it gets hot and this is a clue to the fact that it changes chemically and permanently. You can use a **temperature sensor**, wrapped in cling film, to take readings in the plaster as it sets. How hot does it get? Does the plaster set before it cools down? When does the plaster stop getting warmer? How could you find out if the plaster has really changed? What would happen if you crushed the plaster down to a powder again and added water back to it?

IT: Measuring

Does a burning candle produce water?

When things burn water is made. This is a sign of a chemical change taking place. So paraffin stoves cause condensation and a gas flame produces moisture. You can demonstrate this by burning a candle in a large glass container - the children may see a mist on the cold glass. At the same time you can put a **humidity sensor** in the container - and the computer screen should show a line rising as the candle burns.

IT: Measuring

Dissolving

Which sugar dissolves best?

The children can compare different types of sugar to see which dissolves best. They will need to think carefully about how to make a fair test of the sugars and indeed how they will measure which sugar is best. Should they time how long each sugar takes to dissolve or should they measure how much of each sugar they can dissolve. Either way, they can use a **spreadsheet** program to record their results and produce a bar graph to compare the sugars.

IT: Handling information

Does more sugar dissolve in warm water?

Children can investigate how much sugar dissolves in cold water, tap water and warm water. How much water should they use and how can they make this a fair test? How will they know that no more sugar will dissolve? They can count how many small spoons of sugar dissolve in a certain amount of a water. They will also need to take the temperature of the water. (They ought to take the temperature at the point that no more will dissolve - although it's hard to explain why).

After testing three temperatures they can put the results into a **spreadsheet** table. From this they can produce a scattergraph and be asked: does more sugar dissolve in warm water? Can they use the graph to guess how many spoons dissolve in hot water? How many might dissolve in ice cold water? Does the graph help with the answers? Do they think that if you stirred the cold water more, then more will dissolve?

	A	B	C
1	Dissolving sugar in water		
2	Temperature	How much dissolves	
3	15		
4	21		
5	33		
6	40		

IT: Handling information

Can you identify different sugars?

You can use a **branching database program** to create a 'key' to help you identify different types of sugar. The exercise is a good way of sharpening children's observation too. You collect a set of sugars and the children use them to build up a key on the computer. See the section on branching databases for further details and ideas.

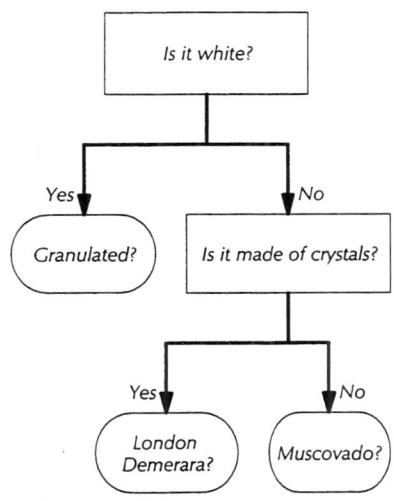

IT: Handling information

What happens to the temperature if you add a pan of cold water to a pan of warm water?

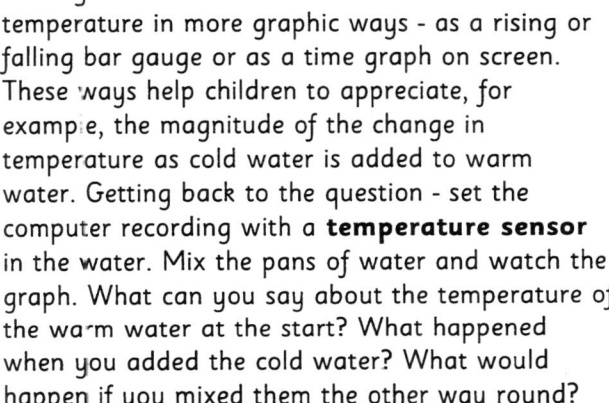

Thermometers are all very well - they are fairly cheap and do not require too much skill to use. However, there are better ways to understand the idea of temperature and temperature changes. **Temperature sensors** linked to the computer allow you to show temperature in more graphic ways - as a rising or falling bar gauge or as a time graph on screen. These ways help children to appreciate, for example, the magnitude of the change in temperature as cold water is added to warm water. Getting back to the question - set the computer recording with a **temperature sensor** in the water. Mix the pans of water and watch the graph. What can you say about the temperature of the warm water at the start? What happened when you added the cold water? What would happen if you mixed them the other way round?

IT: Measuring

What happens to the temperature of a melting ice lolly?

You can freeze the end of a temperature probe inside a block of ice - and take it out of the freezer to record what happens to its temperature as it melts. How long does it take to melt? Does the temperature go up steadily? Or does it change all of a sudden? If you make more temperature probe lollies you might explore further: How can you slow down the melting of your ice lolly? Or, how can you speed up the melting of some frozen soup? How can you make this a fair test?

IT: Measuring

Ideas

Section

3

Using IT in... temperature and energy

Can you guess temperatures correctly?

You might introduce **temperature sensors** with a simple activity such as this: ask the children to record the temperature of various things and places. They can try the radiator, the window, warm water, tap water and their hand. They can measure the temperatures using the computer and record their results on a poster sized thermometer. Can they guess temperatures well? How could they get better at guessing?

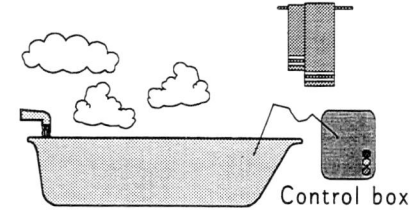

IT: Measuring

Where are the hot spots in the room?

You can use **temperature sensors** to survey the hot and cold spots around the room. This a stepping stone to learning about convection or that hot air rises. You will need to position the computer so that you can take temperatures near the window, the ceiling, the radiator and so on. The differences are slight - usually just a few degrees - but that's still important. They might record the results, by putting red and blue dots on a map of the room. Where did they think the hot spots would be? Can they suggest why some spots are hot and some are cold? What does this tell them about sitting on the floor? Does the room get warmer during the day? Why might this be?

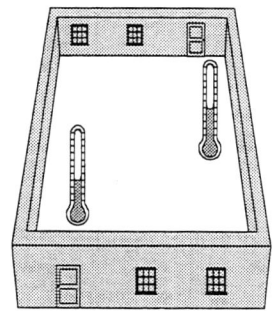

IT: Measuring

Can you make a bath water tester?

You can use your **control box** to make a bath water tester. It might test the temperature of water and tell you whether the water is too hot or too cold - perhaps using coloured warnings lights or buzzers. The children have to write a short control program to run the system, they will need to check it, refine it and evaluate the success of their project.

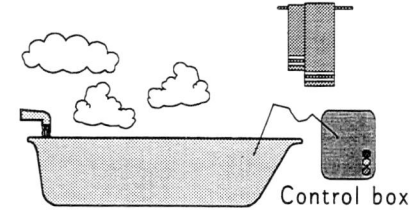

Control box

IT: Control

Can you get a fan to switch on automatically when it gets too hot?

You can use your **control box** to make a cooling fan. A sensor tests the temperature and switches on a fan if it goes too high. It keeps testing the temperature - and when it drops it switches off the fan. You can try other ideas - none are as difficult as they sound: make a sun-seeking solar panel, make a thermostatically controlled greenhouse or aquarium. See the Control section.

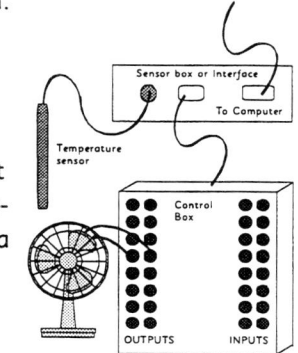

IT: Control

Using IT in... temperature and energy

Do we waste heat in school?

The children can do a survey of temperatures around the school. Are any rooms hotter than they need to be? Are any of the rooms rarely used but still heated? Does the school waste heat? The children can record their results in a **spreadsheet** program. The program provides a ready-made table for recording results. It can draw a bar graph, to compare the temperature differences around the school: which rooms are too warm? How could the school save heat and money?

	A	B	C	D
1	Room temperature survey			
2	Room	Temperature		
3	Red class			
4	Store			
5	Green class			
6	Library			

IT: Handling information

Is the school heating coming on and going off at the best times?

You can monitor the temperature of the room overnight using **temperature sensors**. Set up your system to record for as long as you need to and think about where to place your sensors. If you have two temperature sensors you could put one over the radiator and the other in the room. Get the children to look at the graph: when does the heating come on? When does the room reach a steady temperature? Should we switch the heating on a bit later? When does the heating go off? How long does it take for the room to cool down? Should we switch the heating off a bit earlier?

IT: Measuring

Does perfume make your skin cold or does it just feel cold?

Liquids cool the skin as they dry or evaporate. You can monitor this cooling with a **temperature sensor** - dripping some of the liquid onto the probe and seeing how the temperature drops over a minute. Which cools more, water or after-shave? What does the graph tell you: follow the graph line with your finger and say what is happening. Would blowing on the liquid (i.e. drying it faster) make the temperature go up or go down? How would you feel if you got out of a warm pool and the wind was blowing?

IT: Measuring

Why do your gloves feel so cold when they get wet? Do plastic covered gloves work any better?

When the wind blows over wet gloves, the water evaporates and cools them. You can place **temperature sensors** inside two gloves - one wet and one dry - and monitor the temperature change on the computer. How will you simulate the wind blowing? Which glove cools fastest? Did the wind make any difference? Are waterproof gloves any better? You might repeat the activity with two wet gloves, one in a polythene bag and one uncovered. Which glove stays at the same temperature? What has stopped it from cooling?

IT: Measuring

Ideas

Section

3

Using IT in... temperature and energy

Conduction & radiation

At the seaside, does the sand or the sea warm faster?

Use two **temperature sensors** to compare the temperatures of a bowl of sand and a bowl of water left under a lamp. This shows that 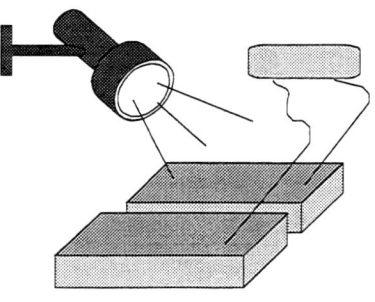 the sun 'gives' energy to the earth - and that some things warm up more easily that others. You will get two graph lines, one for sand and one for the sea. Which line is 'the sea'? What happens to the sand? Which gets the warmest? Would it cool faster? How could you find out?

IT: Measuring

Which material is best for garden chairs?

You can use **temperature sensors** to compare the temperatures of materials - metal, cloth or plastic placed under a lamp. What things are important to make this a good test? The distance from the lamp? Where you place the temperature sensors? How big the material samples are?

IT: Measuring

Which colour clothing is best to wear in hot weather?

Different colours absorb more or less heat and you can use **temperature sensors** to investigate this. You are unlikely to show much difference in heat gained with different coloured fabrics - you will have more success comparing 'coke' cans spray painted different colours - see next item.

IT: Measuring

Which gets hotter in the sun: a red chocolate van or a yellow chocolate van?

When the sun shines, its radiation warms things. And that includes things like chocolate vans. Why is this a problem? Do you think the colour of the van makes a difference? Which colour do you think will be coolest? A good way of finding out which colour absorbs the least heat is to spray paint 'coke' cans different colours. You then place **temperature sensors** in each and arrange them carefully under a desk lamp. The computer will show you that the darker colour warms faster. Would a silver lorry be better?

IT: Measuring

Using IT in... temperature and energy

More heat transfer

If you were heating water should you use a big pan or a small pan?

Which cools down faster, adults or babies?

A teacher took a hot drink to her bath. She dozed off and woke up to find the drink cold but the bath was still warm. What happened?

A teacher made some tea but was called away. Should she add the milk before she goes or after she gets back?

What is the best way to make your hot drink cooler?

You can take an investigative approach to these activities, all of which compare large and small things being heated or being left to cool. There are useful ideas here: large things require more heat to warm them and small things cool faster than large things.

You can solve the 'milk in tea problem' using sensors. You compare the temperatures of two cups of tea, one made with milk added straight away, the other with milk added after several minutes.

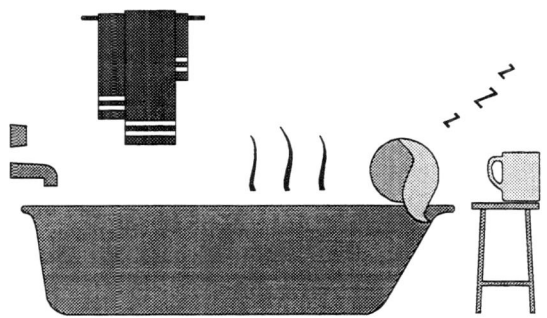

IT: Measuring

Comparing fuels

Which fuel would give you a cup of tea the quickest?

Different fuels give different amounts of energy when they burn. You can compare the heat from a candle and a spirit burner and heat a small tin of water. You can also use sensors to display the temperature changes in the heated tins. What will make this a fair test? The same amounts of water? The same size tins? Look at your graphs, which is which fuel? Which heats things up faster?

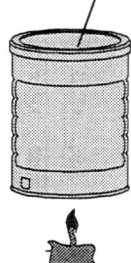

IT: Measuring

Using IT in... temperature and energy

Comparing insulation

Which fabric keeps you warmest?

You go inside after being out in the cold. Would you warm up quicker with your coat on or off?

Materials: which would be best to use as an oven glove?

Cups: which would keep your coffee warm?

Cups: which will help soup cool the fastest?

Teapots: which keeps the tea hot best?

Tea cosies: which keeps the tea hot?

Pizza boxes: which type should they use?

How long does a can of drink from the fridge take to get warm? How can we keep it cool?

How can you keep a bottle of milk cold without a fridge?

Does double glazing work?

Some materials prevent heat transfer better than others. The choice of material is of great importance in keeping us, our houses, our cups of tea and our food at a good temperature. Strangely, heat insulators not only keep things warm, they also keep them cool. **Temperature sensors** connected to the computer are especially useful in this theme. The investigations above require many temperature readings, and sensors linked to the computer take these readings automatically. If nothing else, this allows children to focus on their work and better appreciate temperature changes.

The children need to think about ways to make these investigations fair. They need to take care if you are using hot water - and it would be better that children learn to use sensors in less hazardous activities.

IT: Measuring

Power

How good a solar collector can you make?

You can make a solar collector using an umbrella lined with cooking foil. You can use a **temperature sensor** to find the hot spot on the solar collector. You can point the umbrella towards the sun and move the sensor along the umbrella stem until you find the hottest spot. Does your solar collector work when the sun disappears? How does it perform over an hour?

IT: Measuring

Who can make the fastest windmill?

The children can make windmills using different designs of vane. They can fix it to a **rotation sensor** to measure how fast they turn. Why do some windmills turn faster? The better the vanes, and the less friction in the design the more the wheels should turn.

IT: Measuring

Ideas

Section

3

Using IT in... electricity

Electric circuits

Make an electrical quiz board

Making an electrical quiz board is a nice reinforcement of electric circuit work. This is a small board with a list of questions on one side, a list of answers on the other and wires which

connect each question to an answer. If you choose the right answer a buzzer will sound. Writing sets of questions and answers takes some thought and planning so use a **word processor** to prepare the quiz board. The program will let you make a table with questions and answers, that you can use as a quizboard.

IT: Communicating

Can you draw your circuit so that someone else could make it?

Children have great difficulty producing clearly drawn electric circuits. It's hard to draw the symbols and hard to get them lined up.
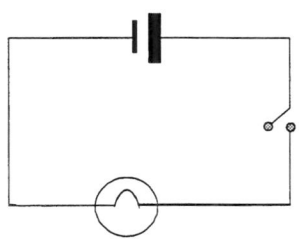
However, a **drawing program** can be useful here - you make the symbols the children need and save this on disk. They can then use this to make their circuits. They will also need to learn to copy and rotate the symbols to draw some circuits, but this is not very hard.

IT: Communicating

Varying current

How does the brightness of a bulb change?

Many questions arise from building electric circuits: does the brightness of a bulb change if you use more batteries? Does the brightness change if you use two bulbs instead of one? Does the brightness change with older batteries? You can extend the work and
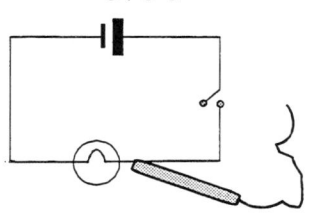
actually measure how bright the bulb is with a **light sensor** attached to the computer. Place the light sensor in a card tube to shield it from light in the room.

IT: Measuring

Electrical hazards

How can we be safe with electricity?

There is a classic exercise where the children look at a picture of a room and try to spot the electrical hazards. For this you can put a picture on an **overlay keyboard** and the children press on a hazard in the picture and get some useful information. You can make these overlays yourself or buy them ready prepared. This example was taken from **Supporting Science** (BECTA)

The program, **Safety First** (Age 8+, Arc/PC from UE) has an easy section on electrical safety. The children have to identify hazards in home situations and score points for this. While it is not that exciting, it adds a little fun.

IT: Modelling

Ideas

Section
3

Using IT in... electricity

Electrical appliances

Which room has the most things that use electricity?

The children can do a survey of the things that use electricity as a nice topic starting activity. They put their findings in a **spreadsheet** table and draw a bar graph of their results. In the graph each bar shows the number of appliances in a room. They can look at the graph to find out which room has the most appliances: are the rooms with the most things the most used?

	A	B	C
1	Electrical equipment survey		
2	Room	How many items with plugs	
3	Red class		
4	Store		
5	Green class		
6	Library		

How important is electricity to us?

Get the children to record the things that they would have to stop doing if there was a power cut. They can say what they would use if say, the lights went out. They can list all these in a tidy **word processor** table.

You might get the children to write a newspaper story about the day there was a power cut. Again, they can use the word processor and go on to present the story, with a picture, in a newspaper layout.

IT: Communicating

Appliances and machines

How does it work?

Using a CD-ROM you can find out about the appliances and machines we use daily. Dorling Kindersley's **The way things work** (age 10-16, CD-ROM PC/Mac from AVP) has some useful ideas for explaining things. The book of the same name is also good. Using either, it's easy to do a project about the refrigerator, how it works, who invented it and so on. Another title, **Inventors and Inventions** (CD-ROM for PC/Arc from The British Library) takes you through machines and their inventors but with fewer thrills.

IT: Modelling

Invent something

Control technology allows children to design systems that work automatically. It is enthralling and gives them an insight into how things work. They could design and build a robot, a buggy, a washing machine, car park barrier, pelican crossing or railway crossing. They can use glue, card, wood, 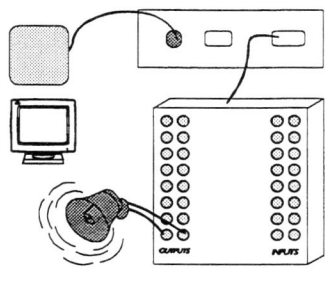 wires, bulbs, motors, switches and sensors. And you can intervene, asking them to explain their designs, or say how what they could make it better and so on. Electricity is a good topic for control projects as the children can exercise their understanding of circuits.

IT: Control

Using IT in... electricity

Cost of electricity

How can we save money on electricity?

You can point children to the 'rating plate' found at the back of many electrical appliances which shows how much power is used. They can carefully collect the power figures from various appliances. They can also record approximately how long each appliance is used for daily. Then, using a **spreadsheet** program, you set up a special recording table. The children enter their figures into the table and it will calculate how much each item costs to run. You might ask: which appliances use the most power? Which are used for the longest time? Which costs the most to run each day? How much does it cost to run the whole house for a day? Some children will be able to see how changing values in the table also changes the electricity bill. By doing this they can answer the question: how much money can we save by switching off the lights?

> See the spreadsheet topic

The program **At Home with Wattville** (BBC/PC/Arc from Understanding Electricity) allows the children to explore the uses and the cost of electricity. They can move round a house and switch appliances on and off. They can pop under the stairs and check the meter. This is a nice easy to understand 'model' of using electricity. The software comes with teaching materials.

IT: Modelling

Making electricity

How can a bicycle make electricity?

A bicycle with a dynamo is a nice model of how electricity is generated. The wheel turns and the lamp lights, but how does the speed of the wheel affect the brightness of the lamp? Computer sensors allow you to answer this in detail: you point a **light sensor** at the lamp and show the light level, as a bar gauge on the computer. If you turn the wheel faster you can measure the difference and, if you also have a **rotation sensor** you can use that to show the speed of the wheel too.

IT: Measuring

Electromagnets

Can we make a strong electromagnet?

You can make an electromagnet by neatly wrapping insulated wire round a large nail. If you connect this to a battery or two the nail will pick up staples - the more staples, the more powerful it may be. This leads to some questions: how can you make the magnet stronger? How can you test how strong it is? The children might try powering the electromagnet with one, two or three batteries and count the number of staples picked up. Or they might see how the number of turns of wire on the nail affects the magnet's strength.

They can put their results into a **spreadsheet** - a program which provides a ready-made table. They can use the spreadsheet to plot a bar graph with the number of batteries along the bottom and the number of staples picked up on the side. Can they see a steady increase in each bar? What does this tell them about using more batteries?

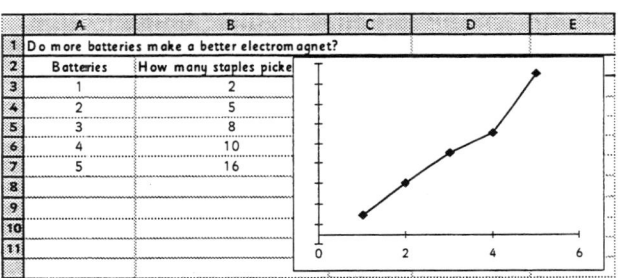

They can investigate the number of turns of wire but this is 'a continuous variable', so it is better to draw a scattergraph. This is harder. This graph should show the number of turns along the bottom and the number of staples picked up on the side. Ask the children if they can 'see' a line through the scatterpoints. If so, they have found a pattern. Would more turns make an even stronger electromagnet? How could they make an electromagnet to pick up a car?

IT: Handling information

Ideas

Section

3

Faster and slower

How can trapeze artists work safely?

Trapeze artists rely on split second timing - and the lengths of the ropes, just like a pendulum is important. Get the children to make a trapeze and ask them to explore its swing. They might say, count how many times it swings in 30 seconds, see if this is always the same and see if the size of the 'artist' affects it. They can use a **spreadsheet** table to record their results and make a bar graph. They can go on to see what happens with a longer rope and compare the graphs. What does this tell you about the trapeze swing?

	A	B	C	D
1	Trapeze	How many swings		
2	Length	Try 1	Try 2	Try 3
3	20			
4	30			
5	40			

Another question, 'which will rolls further, a large cylinder or a small cylinder' provides an opportunity for children to measure, record and look for patterns. They can roll different tubes down a slope and see how far they travel along the floor. They can compare heavy and light tubes, large and small tubes and record their results in a **spreadsheet** or **database program**. They should take a few readings each time to be sure. Using the computer they can start to analyse their results: sort the results into order, which tube rolls further? Draw a bar graph for the different tubes: do larger tubes roll further? What affects how far a tube will travel?

IT: Handling information

Reaction timing

How fast are your reactions?

Children can measure their reaction times very accurately using the computer. You connect two **pressure mats** into your sensor box, and when the children jump on the mats the computer will measure the time between jumps. Other sensors called **light gates** or light switches allow you to measure reaction time too. The children will also gain some computer skills which will be useful for many other timing activities.

IT: Measuring

How fast can you karate chop?

In a way, similar to measuring reaction times above, the children can measure the time of their karate chop using **pressure mats**, **light gates** or light switches. These are sensors that respond to an event, such as a hand passing over them, while the computer measures the time it takes. The activity will provide good practice in measuring, recording and thinking about times and speeds. It may also generate too much excitement - so you might instead try 'how fast can you kick a ball?'.

IT: Measuring

Ideas

Section

3

Using IT in... forces

Pushes and pulls

Which car is the fastest?

It is very different to time, say a toy car moving along the floor. Using **light gates** and light switches connected to your sensor box the task is easy, the results are reliable and a whole range of science activities opens up. Here children will learn about time and speed as they time their cars: which car is the fastest? What must you do to make the car move? When you test the cars will you push them or just release them? Does the size of your push make a difference? Can you make sure that you push the same every time?

IT: Measuring

Forces and the shapes of things

How big a crater would a falling meteor make?

The further a stone falls, the more energy it gives to the ground. The children can investigate this idea by dropping a round object and measuring the dent it makes in a tray of sand. They can record the heights and the dents in a **spreadsheet**, and then plot a scattergraph to see if there is a connection between the two. You might ask: what happens to the crater if you drop from higher up? Can you repeat your results and get the same answer?

Another way to make a similar point is to drop a ball of Plasticene onto the floor from different heights - but this time, the children measure the size of the 'flat' on the Plasticene. Either way, this is a good exercise in measuring and recording.

	A	B	C
1	Making craters		
2	Height	Dent 1	Dent 2
3	20		
4	40		
5	60		

IT: Handling information

Which ball bounces highest?

A ball bouncing tells us that the ball has stored energy. You can get the children to drop a ball and try to measure how high it bounces. Ask them if they can get the same answer each time. Then get them to test balls of different sizes and to enter how high they bounce into a **spreadsheet**. They can draw a bar graph and find out which ball bounces highest. They can also find out if large or small balls bounce best. Or you can get them to see why sports people keep the ball in the fridge.

	A	B	C	D	E	F	G
1	What affects the bounce of a ball?						
2	Ball	Try	Try	Try	Try	Average	Diameter
3	A						
4	B						

IT: Handling information

Attraction and repulsion

Which magnet is the strongest?

The children can test a set of magnets to see which shows the greatest attraction force. They might do this by adding paper clips to a magnet and seeing how many it can pick up or how long a paper clip chain it can hold. Or they could tie a tack on a thread and move the magnet nearer - the stronger the magnet, the greater the distance it works over. They can use a **spreadsheet** to record their findings as well as display these as a graph. You might ask: which magnet is the strongest? How does the graph show this? Can you sort the magnets into two groups, strong and weak? Are pure metal magnets stronger or weaker than ceramic magnets?

IT: Handling information

Using IT in... forces

Gravity

What do things weigh on the moon?

You can use a forcemeter to measure the weight of different objects. It measures the pull of gravity or the gravity force on an object - which is much less (one sixth) on the moon. Your results can be recorded in a **spreadsheet** and the program can be used to calculate how much things weigh on the moon. To do this you enter a formula to divide the earth weight by six. What can the children say about the weight of things on the moon? What would a kilo of sugar weigh on the moon? And what would you weigh? Enter your weight on the spreadsheet to find out.

See the spreadsheet topic

How long does a jump in the air take?

The children can measure the time of a jump in the air using a **pressure mat**. This is a sensor that responds to an event, such as a foot pressing on it, while the computer measures the time taken. The activity will provide good practice in measuring and once you have got the technique, you can find out who can jump and stay in the air the longest.

IT: Measuring

Which will fall faster, a lump of metal or a lump of wood?

Other things being equal, objects fall to earth and land at the same time. It is fun to drop things such as eggs and fruit from windows to see if this is true. But you can also use **pressure mats**, **light gates** or light switches connected into your sensor box and actually measure the fall time.

IT: Measuring

How does the slope of a hill affect the speed of a car?

As above, you can again use **light gates** or light switches. These connect into your sensor box and allow you to measure the time taken for a toy car to roll past the sensor. You can try this at different 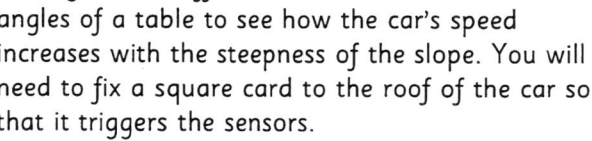 angles of a table to see how the car's speed increases with the steepness of the slope. You will need to fix a square card to the roof of the car so that it triggers the sensors.

IT: Measuring

Does a car speed up as it rolls down a hill?

As a car rolls down a hill it speeds up because of gravity. Use **light gates** or light switches connected into your sensor box and measure the speed of a toy car at different places along a table. The speeds should increase as you measure them further down the slope.

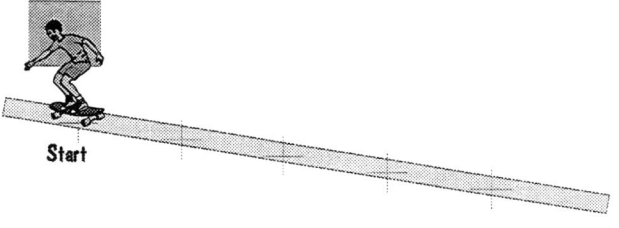
Start

IT: Measuring

Using IT in... forces

How much pulling must you do to move brick?

The friction, or friction force of a surface will affect how easy it is to pull a brick along it. You can use a force meter and 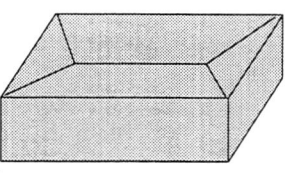 string to pull a brick over carpet, wood, drinking straws, marbles and measure the force needed. The results can be recorded in a **spreadsheet** and turned into a bar graph very easily. You can point the children to the graph and ask: which surface needs the least force to pull the brick? Which surfaces are almost the same? What is it about the surface that makes it hard to pull the brick? What can they do to change this? How would oil, or grease or margarine on the surface change it?

	A	B			G
1	Friction on different surfaces				
2	Surface	Distance travelle			
3	Glass	60			
4	Vinyl	45			
5	Carpet	20			
6	Wood	40			
7	Alumin	50			
8					

Friction experiment: Glass 60, Vinyl 45, Carpet 20, Wood 40, Alumin 50

Similarly, the children can graph how much force it takes to pull a chair over carpet, paper and vinyl. Does it take more force to move it over some surfaces? They can use their forcemeter to record how much force is needed to move different things in the room. Why do different things need different amounts of force?

IT: Handling information

How does the surface affect how far a toy car travels?

A surface can transfer some of the energy of a car rolling down a slope. The friction force reduces the energy of the moving car. You can get the children to see the effect of different surfaces - and they can use a **spreadsheet** to record and graph how far the car goes. If you have **light gates** or light switches for your sensor box, the children could instead measure the speed of a car as it rolls down different surfaces. Which surfaces are the best? Do you think a real car would use less petrol on a smoother road? What is not so good about a smooth road?

IT: Measuring

Should granny wear trainers in poor weather?

As with the brick activity above, the children might test a number of shoes to see which have the most grip. You might ask how they might get a  wet surface and what they will do about shoes that are heavier than others. Again they can use a spreadsheet to record their results. They can sort their shoes into order and draw a bar graph to answer: which shoes are the most grippy?

IT: Handling information

How big a load can a balloon-rocket carry?

You can make a balloon-rocket by threading string through a straw taped to a balloon. Get the children to investigate how different loads, or different lengths of straw affect its movement. Then get them to record and graph their results using a **spreadsheet**. Does the length of the straw affect the rocket? How does the graph tell you this? Does the load affect the rocket? Why might this be?

IT: Handling information

Ideas

Section

3

Using IT in... forces

Which clothes peg can carry the heaviest clothes?

Ask the children to say whether different clothes pegs will carry a lot or a little. Then, in a fair-testing situation, get them to try each peg - they might for example, peg a sock and add weights to the sock. Get them to record your results in a **spreadsheet** and to use it to sort the pegs into order and draw a bar graph. Which peg would they use to hang a wet pair of jeans? Can they spot a good peg?

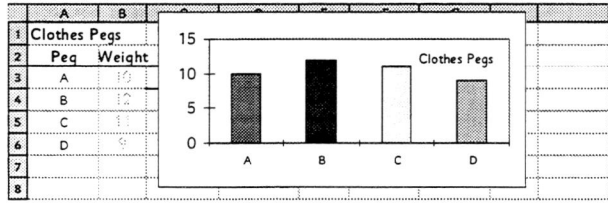

IT: Handling information

How can we warm our hands on a cold day?

If we rub our hands the effort we use creating friction generates heat. You can show this very clearly by holding a **temperature sensor**, connected to the computer, in your hand. The screen will show this as a moving bar or as a line graph. If you have two **temperature sensors** you can make a race of 'warming the sensors' - a fun way of introducing the children to sensors.

IT: Measuring

Which material makes a good parachute?

The parachute is good for teaching about air resistance and the children can set about testing a few. They might use different fabrics, a paper plate, a balloon or a serviette. They might try them with and without a hole in the top. Timing the parachutes is not easy and you might reasonably ask if their tests have been fair and whether they could repeat their results and get the same answer. They can use a **spreadsheet** to record the time each 'chute takes to fall. And they can sort the list and draw a bar graph to compare the parachutes. Are larger parachutes better? Is there a connection between the size of the parachute and the time it takes to fall? Does a hole in the top help?

	A	B	C	
1	Parachute testing	Fall time		
2	Baloon	6		
3	Plate	3		
4	Serviette	10		
5	Nylon	5		

IT: Handling information

Using IT in... forces

What makes a good paper 'plane?

Designing and testing paper planes is a fun way to stimulate interest in the science of flight. There are even computer programs that will print paper templates to make planes (**Paper Planes** and **Aviation** for PC - mail order). But that aside, you can take a design and investigate how the position of the wings, or the position of a weight affects how well the plane can fly. You might time how long they can stay in the air - just be prepared to practice doing this, as it is tricky. You can enter the results into a **database program** and then use it to analyse the results. The children can sort the results to find the best plane. Should the plane have weights on the nose? Some children could plot a scattergraph of wing position against the distance travelled - and find a pattern here.

	A	B	C
1	Plane testing	Wing position	Fly time
2	Mine		
3	Hers		
4	Theirs		

Instead of 'planes they can make paper spinners or gyroplanes. They can try different size wings, different wing cut-aways, or different numbers of paper clip weights, and they can time how long each design takes to fall. Again a **database program** will help them to handle the results. They can select out the spinners with long wings and see whether those with more clips spin best. They can draw a bar graph, and write on their ideas, about what makes a good spinner, on the print-out.

IT: Handling information

Elastic band power

Make and test a launcher for a dart plane

The children can make an elastic launcher for a paper plane and investigate the best way to use it. How could they test it scientifically? Should they use a ruler to measure how much they pull the elastic band? They could try a number of firing positions and record how far their plane flies in a **spreadsheet**. The program can draw a bar graph of their results. What does the graph tell them? Is it best to pull the elastic all the way back?

Alternative: who can make the best catapult to throw a paper ball? Does the size of the paper ball affect how far it travels?

IT: Handling information

Which elastic band is the strongest?

A nice investigation, involving some information handling arises from the design of an elastic band tester. They can tie a band to a hook and then to a bulldog clip. The children can test how far the band stretches with more and more weight attached. They can use a **spreadsheet** to record and bar graph their results. You might ask: what pulls on the band? Does gravity pull more on a large weight or a small weight? Is there a pattern between the weight and the stretch?

Who can make a good elastic band roller?

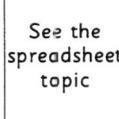
See the spreadsheet topic

All sorts of elastic band devices can be used for investigations on energy. There are cotton-reel rollers, buggies and planes any of which can be tested to show that the more energy we give to the elastic, the more the devices can travel. Ask the children to find a way of testing this idea. Get them to use a **spreadsheet** to record their results. Which type of graph best shows their results? Why does winding more make it go further?

IT: Handling information

Using IT in... forces

Direction of forces

Which is the best angle for a firework rocket launch?

The children can make an elastic launcher and investigate the best angle to use it. They might use a protractor to measure the launching angle. They could try a number of angles and use a **spreadsheet** to record how far their projectile flies. The program will help them to draw a bar graph. Is there a best angle? Is the best angle, the biggest angle? If they wanted to throw a ball a long way, what should they remember?

	A	B	C	D	
1	Which is the best launch angle?				
2	Angle	Try	Try	Try	A
3	10				
4	20				
5	30				
6	40				
7	50				

Alternatively they can investigate 'the human cannon ball'. Does the angle of the cannon matter? Does the length of the cannon barrel affect how far the ball travels? Does the weight of the human cannon ball matter?

IT: Handling information

Balancing forces

Which is the strongest type of bridge?

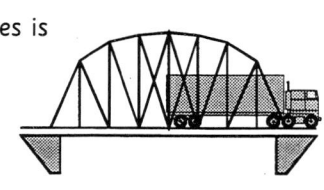

Making and testing bridges is an opportunity for 'fair tests' and learning about structures. The children can test bridge shapes which are flat, round, box and fluted. They can take one design and test it with different spans. Or take a flat design and try it with different size arches.. They can load their bridges with weights and record their results. A **spreadsheet** provides a ready-made table for this and it can sort their bridges in order and draw a bar graph to compare the various designs. You can ask the children which bridge is the strongest. Is it the best by far or by just a bit? Can they divide the bridges into strong and weak types? How does the graph help them to do this?

When the children have chosen the best bridge design, they could make it stronger still - they might make a bridge with one, two, three or more pieces of card. It's a real engineer's problem, but when should they stop trying to make the bridge stronger? They can test their bridges as before, and graph their results in a **spreadsheet**. Does more card make the bridge stronger? Does more card make a lot of difference? Can they use the graph to guess how much weight a bridge with even more card would take?

> See the spreadsheet topic

IT: Handling information

Which boat will carry the most?

The children can test boats made from aluminium trays or margarine tubs to see which will carry the most. They can use a **spreadsheet** to record and graph their results. Do larger boats carry more? Do shallow boats carry less? Do light boats carry less? The children may think that the weight of a boat's load is not important, so maybe they can investigate further: would a full boat sail as fast as an empty boat?

IT: Handling information

Using IT in... forces

What floats and what sinks?

Test some things to see if they float or sink. Use a forcemeter to measure their weight in air and their weight in water - the floaters should weigh nothing in water. Record the results in a **spreadsheet** table - do not graph the weights.

IT: Handling information

How does the pressure change when you squash things?

You can show how pressure changes when balloons are squashed with the help of a **pressure sensor**. You attach this, quite costly, sensor to a balloon and then squash the balloon. The computer screen will show you the effect as a bar gauge on the screen. It should show how squashing and pressure are connected.

Using the same set-up you can show how pressure changes with the depth of water - an important point for divers and submarines, because the deeper they go the stronger their equipment must be. Older pupils may be able to measure the depth, record the pressure and see if there is a pattern between them.

IT: Measuring

Machines

A **control box** allows children to make machines that work automatically. It gives them an insight into how things work. They can build a fork-lift truck, a buggy, a conveyor belt, a car park barrier, drilling machine or a railway crossing. They can build the system using glue, card, wood, wires, bulbs, motors, switches and sensors. Control technology is an excellent context for children to think about energy, gears, structures and using information technology.

IT: Control

Explore the different types of machines using Dorling Kindersley's lovely **The Way things Work** (age 10-16, CD-ROM for PC/Mac on mail order). Record your findings in a table on your **word processor**. The word processor helps by allowing the children to work as a team and by allowing them to edit their writing as their ideas develop. There is an interesting invention time line on the CD-ROM and the children could take notes from this and produce their own, using the graphing features of a **spreadsheet**.
Usborne Exploring Science: Physics (age 8-14, CD-RCM Archimedes from Hampshire) has illustrations from the Usborne books 'Things that Move' and 'Everyday things' and deals with science in the everyday world".

IT: Communicating

Find out about...

Using IT in... light

Light travels from a source

How far will the light from a candle travel?

You can use a **light sensor** to show how much light comes from a candle. The computer can display the light level as a number or a bar display on the screen. The children can place the sensor in a cardboard tube to 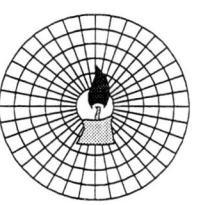 make it directional. Move the sensor away from a lit candle and find out: is there a point where the sensor no longer picks up light from the candle? What does the computer show? Why does the light level drop as you move further away? Is candle light brighter in the dark?

IT: Measuring

Which light source is the best to read by?

You can use a **light sensor** to investigate the brightness of different light sources. The children can do a fair test of a candle, a torch, a striplight and a desk lamp. They need to keep the distance from the light source the same and avoid extraneous light. What are the advantages of each light source?

| See the sensors topic |

IT: Measuring

Which candle gives off the most light?

You can use a **light sensor** to investigate the brightness of different candles. The children can try to test the candles fairly and find out: do long candles give off more light than short candles? Do fat candles give off more light than thin candles?

IT: Measuring

Which are the brightest and the darkest places in the room?

We see things because light comes from a source and the children can use a **light sensor** to do a survey of the light in the room. They can record the results on a map of the room. Why are the lightest places light? Where does the light come from? Why are the darkest places dark? Why can't we see well in dark places?

IT: Measuring

Light enters our eyes

How do we see?

How is the **light sensor** like our eye? How can the computer see light? You can use a light sensor as a model of the human eye. The light sensor has a light sensitive part just as we have a retina. It has wires that take messages to the computer for processing - just as we have nerves that take messages to our brain.

IT: Modelling

Ideas

Section

3

Using IT in... light

Light is reflected from surfaces

Is the light from a candle the same from every angle? Is the light from a torch the same from every angle?

Candles provide general light while a torch has a 'directional' beam. The children can use a **light sensor** to take light readings at different angles around a torch and a candle. You might ask: when would a candle be useful? What makes a torch directional? How could you make a candle beam like a torch beam? How could you make a torch beam like a candle?

IT: Measuring

What happens when light shines on things?

Some light is absorbed when it is reflected from a table, a mirror and even day-glo material. The children measure the light reflected from a table by pointing a **light sensor** at it. They can find out which surfaces reflect the most light. They can sort them into order: which reflects the most light?

IT: Measuring

Light passes through different materials

What is the best material for a window blind?

You can use a **light sensor** to see how much light can pass through different materials. The children put the sensor in a box with a 'window' at one 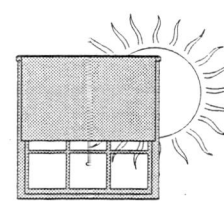 end. They put different fabrics or materials over the window. The computer will show how transparent the material is. Do your results help you to sort out the materials? Which materials are transparent? Which are opaque? Which are translucent? Which would be best for a window blind? Would thicker materials let through less light? How many layers of tracing paper would stop the light getting through?

IT: Measuring

Does light travel through water?

You can take light level readings in a pond. You need to place the **light sensor** in a well-sealed plastic bag. You can show how the light level affects the life in different parts of the pond. You will need a portable computer or plug your sensor into a data logger. Remember to always point the sensor at the same angle (up is best) or you will get spurious readings.

IT: Measuring

How fast do photochromic sunglasses change?

You can use a **light sensor** to investigate how fast photochromic glasses (which darken in the sun) change. The children can place the sensor in a card tube and measure the light passing through the lens. Can they predict what  will happen? The computer will display a graph showing the lenses getting dark or light. Can they predict what the computer screen will show? Do the glasses get darker, faster than they get lighter? When would it be important that the glasses change fast?

IT: Measuring

Using IT in... light

Comparing colours

Which colour fabric is best for a cyclist to wear?

Light is 'lost' or absorbed when it is reflected from different coloured surfaces. Day-glo materials do this less. The children can measure the light reflected from coloured fabrics by pointing a **light sensor** at it. Sort the colours into order. Which colours would be best for the cyclist? Which fabric reflects the most light - a plain yellow or day-glo yellow?

See the sensors topic

Note: The light sensor responds to different colours in a way not exactly like the human eye. For this reason, and because different surfaces reflect light differently, results should be seen as 'rough and ready'.

IT: Measuring

Which colour sunglasses filter light best?

Coloured film filters out some of the light passing through them. The children can use a **light sensor** to compare the amount of light passing through different coloured sunglasses made using coloured film. Which colour will work best? Would you buy your clothes wearing sunglasses? See if you can guess the colours of clothes wearing different sunglasses.

IT: Measuring

Which colours are the safest colours for the road?

As above, you can measure the light reflected from coloured material by pointing a **light sensor** at it. And the children can use the light sensor to compare paint swatches from DIY shops. You might ask: Which colours would be best for road signs? Which colours would be best for the crossing patrol, or a police car? Would the time of day affect the results?

IT: Measuring

What happens when we mix coloured lights?

Dorling Kindersley's CD-ROM title **The Way Things Work** (PC/Mac on mail order) features a lovely graphic 'model' of mixing coloured light.

Using light

How does it work?

Dorling Kindersley's CD-ROM title **The Way Things Work** (PC/Mac on mail order), features graphic explanations of how the camera, the telescope and other optical devices work.

Wayland's **Light & Sound** (age 9-14, CDROM for PC/Mac on mail order) is an easy enough tutorial looking at most aspects of light at this level.

IT: Modelling

Ideas

Section

3

Using IT in... sound

Making sounds

Which sound maker is the loudest?

How do the strings on an elastic-band guitar affect the sound?

How does the size of the guitar box affect the sound?

Which rice shaker is the loudest?

What makes a noisy shaker?

Does the amount of rice in a shaker affect the noisiness?

If you drop something from higher up does it make a louder sound?

Can you trust your ears to measure sound?

What makes a good drum sound?

Who has the quietest shoes?

The children can investigate making sounds. They can use string, percussion or wind instruments looking at how to make the sound and how to change the pitch or volume. After this initial work, you can introduce the pupils to the **sound sensor** - a device which allows them to measure, rather than guess-at how loud a sound is. They can display the readings on the screen to get a more easily understood measure of volume.
The questions above provide some ideas to investigate. They should try to predict sound levels - you might draw a 'noise line' and ask them to write where along it the sound might sit. Although they might test large drums and small drums, sand filled drums and empty drums, large tappers and small tappers, paper skin or plastic skin - they should learn to look at one thing at a time. Note: The sound sensor responds to all noise, so do this somewhere quiet.

Note: The sound sensor responds to different frequencies unevenly and in a way unlike the human ear. For this reason, results should be seen as 'rough and ready'.

IT: Measuring

Kinds of sounds

Can you describe the sound?

Get a cassette tape with different sounds on it and ask a group to describe each sound. Do a brainstorm on the describing words they could use, like banging or clanging, and put the list up on the board. If you have an **overlay** 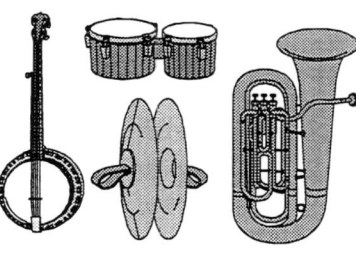 ('concept') keyboard you can prime your **word processor** with such words and the children can use them at the press of a button.

The children can use a 'branching database' program to build up a 'key' to identify each sound. You prime the computer with a couple of instruments - the children add the rest. They will learn how to sort things and observe carefully.

You can create a simple database of musical instruments. The exercise gets children to organise their data: they will need to record what the instrument is, what family it belongs to, how it makes sound, what types of music it is used for and what country it comes from. Books as well as Microsoft's **Musical Instruments** (CD-ROM PC/Mac - mail order) provide plenty of information. Wayland's **Light & Sound** (age 9-14, CDROM for PC/Mac on mail order) is an easy enough tutorial looking at most aspects of sound at this level.

IT: Handling information

Using IT in... sound

Which sounds stop quickly and which stop slowly?

Most brands of **sound sensor** are quite good at showing how fast a sound grows and fades away. This 'attack' and 'decay' idea helps us to distinguish a drum sound, which is short from a flute sound, which is long. Get your sensor software to show a line graph as you make the sounds. Set it to read over a 10 second timespan, as this will show a more detailed graph. The children can look at the graphs and consider: do sounds that last longer have anything else in common? Do the sounds that grow quickly have anything in common? Do high sounds stop more quickly than low sounds?

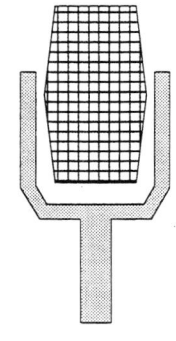

Sound and distance

Does sound fade the further you are from it?

The children can use a sound sensor to see how the sound level changes with distance. They might use an electronic organ or a tape recorder to make a sound. Can they be sure that this sound is the same each time? Over what distances will they measure the sound? Some children will be able to use a **spreadsheet** to record, and produce a bar graph of their results: what does the graph tell them about sound and distance? Why do they think that sounds fade with distance? Where does the sound go?

IT: Measuring

Hearing sound

How do our ears help us collect sound?

The children can listen to a sound with and without an ear trumpet. They can use a **sound sensor**, in place of their ear, and measure how the trumpet affects the sound level. You can ask: does the trumpet increase the sound level? Would a larger trumpet help more? Which animals do you think should be able to hear well? See if some ear shapes work better than others.

IT: Measuring

How do our ears work?

A **sound sensor** is a good 'model' of how the ear works. It is a microphone with a membrane that vibrates in a similar way to the ear drum. Then there are wires, like nerves, to carry a message to the computer (or brain).

IT: Measuring

Ideas

Section

3

Using IT in... sound

Sound and safety

Where is that noise coming from?

The children can do a noise survey with the **sound sensor**. They can measure the noise level in school over the day. With a sensor extension lead or a portable computer they can go outside. Which is the noisiest part of the classroom? Which room is the noisiest? When is the noise worst?

IT: Measuring

Which material would make the best ear muffs for the teacher?

The children can test sound proofing materials by wrapping them round a **sound sensor** to see if they can lower the sound level. You might ask: which material is the better sound proofer? Do extra layers of material help reduce the sound? Where does the sound go? Are high sounds easier to stop than low sounds? Note: They will need a very quiet testing area.

IT: Measuring

Make an alarm which switches off when you shout.

See the control topic

Using a buzzer, a **sound sensor**, a **control box** and sensor box, you can make a sound controlled alarm.

IT: Control

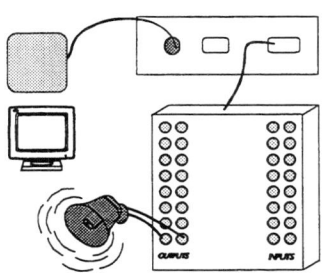

Sound travel

What can sound travel through?

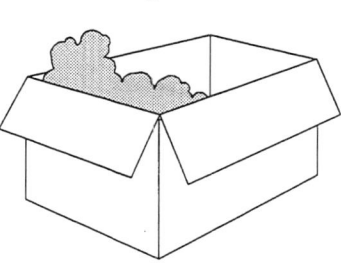

The children can test different materials to see if sound can travel through them. They can press a **sound sensor** onto an object and make a sound at the other end of it. They might test a metal pipe or table leg, a wooden door, a fish tank, a balloon full of water or a balloon full of air. They will need a synthesizer or something that makes a steady sound.

IT: Measuring

Which material makes the best string telephone?

You can investigate sound travelling through string telephones - measuring the sound level in the 'ear cup' with a **sound sensor**. The computer will record the sound level on a graph. They can measure the sound level when they pinch the string, stretch it round a corner. They can also swap the string for wool or wire. You might ask: which materials allow sound to pass easily? How does the sound get from one cup to the other?

IT: Measuring

Using IT in... earth and weather

Looking at rocks

How do we identify rocks?

You can get children to examine a collection of rocks and provide help with describing them. You can use a **word processor** where the important 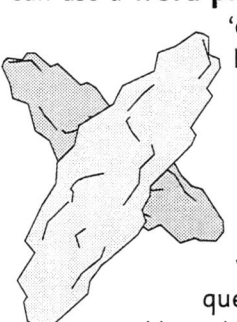 'describing' words like jagged, lumpy, gritty are available by pressing an overlay ('**Concept**') **keyboard**. When the children press on a word, it is typed into the word processor. You can also prime the word processor with

questions like: what colour is the rock? Does it have streaks? Is it rough? 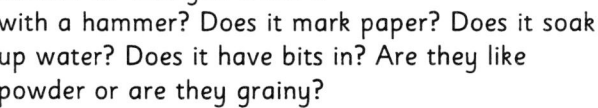 Is it crumbly? Can you scratch it? Can you crush it with a hammer? Does it mark paper? Does it soak up water? Does it have bits in? Are they like powder or are they grainy?

IT: Communication

There is a Rocks and Minerals database you can use with the Key database although something more pictorial, such as a CD-ROM would be helpful. **Exploring Earth Science** (age 10-16, CD-ROM for PC from Attica) covers the structure of the earth as well as the night sky in detail. It is too hard, however.

IT: Handling information

Water cycle

Arrange the steps of the water cycle into order.

You can prepare a sorting exercise using a modern **word processor** program. You type the steps of water cycle in the word processor and put the sentences in the  wrong order. The children then re-arrange the steps into order. You can make a graphical version of this exercise by using the **My World** program (PC/Arc from Semerc) to make a series of mini-pictures or 'sprites' that can be moved around the screen.

IT: Communicating

Using IT in... earth and weather

Weather recording

How the weather changes.

You can use the computer to record the weather in a variety of ways. The easiest is with the **My World** program (PC/Arc from Semerc) which comes with a map you can drop weather symbols onto. You can prepare a daily weather grid and the children can add weather symbols to it.
The well above average **WeatherMapper** program (PC/Arc/Mac from TAG) has useful information on weather, and allows you to record weather data and make weather maps. And you can use a camcorder to record children giving a weather report using the program. For the multimedia treatment **All about Weather and Seasons** (age 5-8, PC/Mac CDROM from SEMERC) has activities and and information. It's likeable.

There are weather stations with instruments you read daily, and others like the **Weather Reporter**, (Advisory Unit) that record the weather automatically. Computer sensors can do this too, not as elegantly but acceptably. A **light sensor** records daylight and sunlight, a **rotation sensor** records the wind speed, a pressure sensor records the barometric pressure and a **temperature sensor** provides the temperature. You might collect enough data to ask whether it's cooler when the wind blows or whether it's warmer when it is bright.

IT: Handling information / Communication

Seasonal changes

How are the seasons different?

You can make a four-box table in a **word processor**, one box for each of the four seasons. The children can fill these in with their ideas. Or they can use a **drawing program** to create a poster about the seasons. They might focus on how the seasons affect our lives. As they work they may come to change their ideas - some say it rains more in winter and others will disagree. The computer acts as a neutral area where children can discuss each other's work.
Climate Change (age 11-16, CD-ROM for Acorn / PC from YI) is about the effects of climate change on the environment - it is easy to use, but the reading level is high.

IT: Communication

Ideas

Section

3

Length of the day and night

When does the day begin and end?

You can use a **light sensor** to record the light levels over 48 hours. A graph on the computer will show rising and falling light levels and you can get the children to look at this: which part of the graph shows day time? Which shows night time? Is there light at night? When does the day begin? When does it end?

IT: Measuring

How do 'lighting-up' times change during the term?

You can collect lighting-up times from a newspaper or almanac and record them in a **spreadsheet** program. You can make a table and a bar graph. The bar graph should show that the times decrease towards June and increase after it.

	A	B	C	D	
1	Sunrise and Sunset				
2	Date	Lights off	Lights on	Length day	Le
3	1/Dec/91	7:45	15:53	8:08	
4	8/Dec/91	7:54	15:49	7:55	
5	15/Dec/91	8:01	15:48	7:47	
6	22/Dec/91	8:06	15:50	7:44	
7	29/Dec/91	8:08	15:55	7:47	

You might also do the same to compare lighting-up times between the North and the South of the country. Get a globe and a lamp (i.e. a sun) and try to predict if it gets darker in the North earlier or later than the South. Does your bar graph agree with your prediction?

IT: Handling information

People ring your door buzzer at night. Make a buzzer that only works during the daytime.

You can use **control technology** to design and make an automated system to do this. You need a buzzer and a **light sensor** and you use the program to check the light level and control when the buzzer works. See the Control section for like examples.

See the control topic

IT: Control

The sun appears to move in the sky

How do shadows tell the time?

You can place a stick in the ground and record the angle or the length of the shadow at set times throughout the day. You can enter your results into a **spreadsheet** program and plot a bar graph. How does the length of the shadow change? How does the angle of the shadow change? Which of these help you to tell the time?

	A	B	C	
1	Shadows			
2	Time	Shadow angle	Shadow length	
3	10:00			
4	11:05			
5	12:00			
6	13:00			

IT: Handling information

Make a solar panel that always points towards the light?

A solar panel is not much good if it's not pointing towards the sun. You can use **control technology** to make a sun-seeking solar panel. It consists of a motorised turntable and two **light sensors**. You write a control program which compares the light level from each sensor and then turns the turntable left or right to point towards the light.

IT: Control

Using IT in... earth and space

Planets orbit the sun

All about the planets

There are legions of television programs, **Internet** pages and CD-ROM resources about space. You can get the children to use a CD-ROM to prepare a travel agent's poster for a holiday on one of the planets - although not many CD-ROM titles are designed specially for a young audience. Nevertheless, you will find pictures of planets, stars and space craft that you can use in poster work and multimedia presentations. You could use the **Interactive Space Encyclopaedia** (age 10+, CD-ROM PC/Mac/Arc on mail order) - a better-than-a-book resource with words, pictures and film of people landing on the moon and so on. While **Red Shift 3** (age 12+, CD-ROM PC/Mac on mail order) is a 'model' that allows children to see the orbits of the planets - it is too technical to really recommend.

Discovering Astronomy and **Solar System Explorer** (age 12+, CD-ROM PC/Mac on mail order) are from the Red Shift people. The first has clips of animation created using Red Shift and although this makes it easier to use, it is still not easy enough. The second puts you in charge of a space ship and lets you visit the planets. This would be good at home where there may be more time to spare.

Better is **Planetary Taxi** (age 9-11, CD-ROM Mac from TAG) where the children learn about the planets as they tour a scale model of the solar system. It also includes video and NASA photographs.

Dorling Kindersley's **Eyewitness Space and The Universe** (age 10+, CD-ROM for PC/Mac on mail order) features a star dome, man on the moon film and really is worth a look. Microsoft's **Magic Bus Explores the Solar System** (CD-ROM PC on mail order) is a great deal of fun and excellently produced, I thought it was too much fun - and better at home. **Learn about the Night Sky** (ages 4-9, Mac from TAG) is worth a look. **Space Shuttle** (11+, CD-ROM for Mac from REM) is for NASA fans only. **Space Adventure II** (age 11-14, CD-ROM for PC on mail order) has games and information - fun but best kept at home. **Earth and Universe** (age 14-16, CD-ROM for PC from BTL) covers much of this subject area - seasons, tides and so on quite well but at a high level - though it is very dry.

For your Acorn computers there are **Astro**, **Astronomy** and **Space Apprentice** (Age 9+, from AVP). **Space Trek** (for Arc from Resource) is a collection of **graphics** and backgrounds which the children can assemble into story books. Part of the **Bookmaker** series, this has planets, astronauts and spacecraft to move around and build a space station or recreate the first landing on the moon.

IT: Modelling

Which is the biggest planet?

You can use a book or CD-ROM to find out about the sizes of the planets and put the data in a **spreadsheet** program. You can sort the list to put the biggest planets at the top. You can also use the program to draw a bar graph and ask: which planet is the biggest? Can you sort the planets into two groups, big planets and small planets. Where did you draw the dividing line between big and small?

IT: Handling information

Using IT in... earth and space

Make an orrery.

You can use a **spreadsheet** to help you construct a model solar system - stretching from one end of the hall to the other. You put values for the distances of each planet into a spreadsheet. In one of the spreadsheet columns you enter a calculation which allows you to scale the planet's real distances from the sun down to the length of the hall. You enter the length of the hall and the computer will work out the correct scale for you. What problem do you face if you make an orrery a table?

	A	B	C
1		Millions of kilometres	cm
2	Pluto	5800	40
3	Neptune	4500	31
4	Uranus	2900	20
5	Saturn	1400	10
6	Jupiter	780	5
7	Mars	230	2
8	Earth	150	1
9	Venus	110	0.8
10	Mercury	60	0.4
11	Sun	0	0

IT: modelling

How do the planets compare?

There are many patterns in data on the planets. You might wonder if there is a pattern between the size of a planet and its distance from the sun, or if larger plants have more moons. A **database program** allows children to explore these patterns easily - in an enjoyably investigative way. You can collect data about each of the planets and type it into the database program. You can see if there is a pattern between the size of a planet and its distance from the sun. You use the computer to plot a scattergraph of size of the planets against distance. If there is a pattern, you will 'see' a line or curve through your scatterpoints. Can find other patterns: is there a pattern between the temperature on the planet and its distance from the sun? Can you explain why?

IT: Handling information

Do you know your planets?

You can play a 20-questions game on the planets - one person thinks of a planet, while the others have to ask questions to guess it. And you can then use a **branching database** program to enter these questions into the computer. This is an absorbing exercise which gets children to make careful observations about the planets.

IT: Handling information

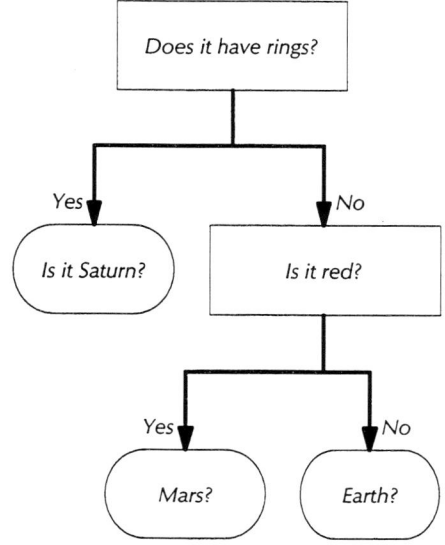

Using IT in... earth and space

The earth orbits the sun with a tilt

Why is summer warmer than winter?

You can illustrate this difficult idea using a desk lamp (the sun) and a globe. You then use **temperature sensors** to record the temperatures at two positions - one with the sun at an angle and one with the sun directly overhead.

IT: Modelling

The phases of the moon

How does the moon change in shape?

You can keep a moon diary using a computer **drawing program**. You draw a grid of boxes like a calendar and then fill in the boxes using moon shapes. The program will allow you to copy shapes you have already drawn - so this gets easier as you work through a month. Once you have completed the grid, you could print it and create a game where the children have to arrange moon shapes into the correct sequence.

Shape of the moon

Monday
Tuesday
Wednesday
Thursday
Friday

Several **CD-ROM** titles explain the phases of the moon fairly graphically. See under planets for recommendations.

IT: Modelling

Life in space

Moon people

Use a **word processor** in a team exercise to make a newspaper front page about the day they landed on the moon. They may be able to illustrate their story with pictures they find in a CD-ROM, a 'clip-art' library or from the **Internet**.

IT: Communication

Do astronauts keep cool in shiny suits?

Use **temperature sensors** to compare the temperatures of astronauts dressed in fabric and in shiny foil suits. Get a desk lamp to shine on wrapped-up bottles. Ask the children: when the sun shines, will your astronauts warm up or cool down? How does the computer graph show you what happened? Do the suits protect them from the sun's heat rays? Which suit material protects best?

IT: Measuring

Ideas

Section

3

Notes

Help

National bodies

The national focus for IT in education is the BECTA or **British Education and Communications Technology Agency**. See Becta's National Grid for Learning for IT and primary science activities. Web **www.becta.org.uk**

Focus for science teaching - the **Association for Science Education**: **www.ase.org.uk**

Also the **National Centre for Initial Teacher Training in Primary Science**, SCIcentre, School of Education, 21 University Road, LE1 7RF Tel 0116 252 3659 Email mw47@leicester.ac.uk

Advice and training

IT in science - Roger Frost at **IT in Science** provide specialist advice. See www.rogerfrost.com

General Science

All about science...

Science Explorer I and II (age 8-11) are full of information and investigations - well written, it is bang on curriculum target. It's something pupils can use to clue up on science in the classroom or library. (CD-ROM for Acorn/Mac/PC from Granada Learning).

Science Fair (age 5-8, CD-ROM for PC/Mac/Acorn from Sherston) is a likeable title to investigate. Good for the infants.

Children's Micropedia (age 8+, CD-ROM Archimedes or PC from TAG) from the **Kingfisher Children's Encyclopaedia** has 1300 entries and 1600 pictures which you can also use in project work. It is very easy to use and well worth a look. **Oxford**

Children's Encyclopaedia (age 9-13) is a quality encyclopaedia for a young UK audience and most recommended to schools. Needs a 1997 computer to run well. (CD-ROM for PC - mail order).

The Random House Kid's Encyclopaedia (age 7-11, CD-ROM for PC on mail order) stuns with fun, has a little on science but is more for US homes.

Microsoft's Encarta (age 12-adult, CD-ROM for PC/Mac - mail order) is good for finding information. It's very attractive, easy to use but the language is too hard for primary children.

Dorling Kindersley's **Eyewitness Encyclopaedia of Science** (age 11-15, CD-ROM for PC/Mac - mail order) is attractive, but is patchy and focuses more on pure rather than applied science - so for swots only. Dorling Kindersley's **First Incredible Amazing Dictionary** (age 5-7) has bits of science - body words for example - and worth having never mind the science.

Hutchinson Multimedia Encyclopaedia (age 11-adult, CD-ROM for Acorn from Attica) is a not very detailed encyclopaedia. The text is hard and complex. It is home-spun which is an advantage in some curriculum areas.

The **Grolier Multimedia Encyclopaedia** (age 12-adult, CD-ROM for PC/Mac - mail order) is easy to use, but the text, as always, is hard.

Compton's Interactive Encyclopaedia (age 12-16, CD-ROM for PC - mail order) is spurious in its coverage and much of a muchness.

CD-ROMs

CD-ROM software for science is listed in the main ideas for topics section of this book. Choose your topic area and look for the bold text where you will find a brief review and details. The positive reviews are clear pointers to what is worth having, less definite ones mean that you should see them before buying. Education 'trade shows' such as the UK **BETT** exhibition and the **ASE** annual meeting (early January) are excellent events to do hands-on shopping. Roger Frost's **Software for Science Teaching** (ASE) is the book with detailed reviews of 'everything' but it's better value for the secondary school. Also see **Using CDROMs in primary Science** - a booklet from National Centre for Initial Teacher Training in Primary Science, SCIcentre, - address on this page.

Some titles were too broad to put under any heading in the Ideas section: **Science Explorer** (see this page) or **Sammy's Science House** (age 4-7, for Mac from **Iona or TAG**) for the early years are among them - both are well above average. SSH looks at weather, the environment, sequencing and classification. There is a construction workshop where you put together structures from bird boxes to helicopters. It's intelligent and ahead of the rest. **Smudge the Scientist** (age 4-7, floppy disc for PC/Arc/Mac from Storm or AVP) has a grow-a-plant simulation, a decay simulation as well as sorting exercises on magnetic or non-magnetic and floaters or sinkers. Not at all bad, not special and looks dated beside others.

Resources

Section

4

For SATs practice see **Practise Science for the National Tests** (age 9-11 for PC/Arc from Granada Learning) which does just what the title says.

Software catalogues

Are available from software suppliers (AVP and TAG). Get the special needs software catalogues from Semerc and Cleveland. General purpose software is available from Microsoft dealers, BlackCat, SPA, Flexible software, Logotron, Kudlian Soft, Computer Concepts, Colton, Claris.

Branching databases

Flexitree (for PC from **Flexible Software**) is a rare breed of program - the branching database. This one is capable and not expensive.The blindingly simple, **Sorting Game** (for BBC from BECTA, for Acorn and Windows from MAPE) still goes strong. **Idelta** (for Nimbus) is no longer available but use it if you have it. Oxford LEA offer **Branch** (DOS PC) which does the business. Kudlian do **Retreeval** (disc for PC/Arc) - which is fine. **Window Tree** (for PC from SITSS) is capable, pricey and may be unobtainable.

Clip-art & multimedia

When children need to illustrate their work, it's good to have a collection of clip-art. Your printer will manage beautiful full colour graphics but photographs may not come out at chemist quality. The professional graphics programs all provide huge collections of this. You could look for titles like **Corel Draw, Art & Letters Express, Page Plus, Micrografx Designer** and **Draw Plus** (all PC on mail order). They are not that expensive but some would say you don't need anything this good. You will find collections of art bundled free with **Microsoft Word, Publisher, Micrografx Draw** and **Claris Works**. You may just need to hunt through the hard disc to find them. Remember that your CD-ROM encyclopedia will often let you clip pictures into your work. The Internet can also be culled for clip art.

To create a multimedia presentation your best bet is **Hyperstudio** (Arc/PC/Mac - from TAG). There is also much to be said for the ease of use offered by **Magpie** (for Arc from Logotron).

Ready-drawn 'clip-art' to illustrate children's work is widely available. Starting places are the **Bitfolio collections** (CD-ROM for Arc/Mac/PC - mail order) and the collections of zoo animals, birds and pond life in **Just Pictures** (PC/Arc/Mac from Semerc). There is **Clip Art CD Collection** (age 7-14 for PC/Arc) from Sherston which has the best set of curriculum use pictures I've seen. Two other education specialists providing clip-art are Anglia Multimedia and Appian Way Software. You can find clip-art packages with thousands of images in retail outlets but do check to see whether it has what you need. Multimedia programs allow children to assemble text, pictures and video and make a multimedia presentation. These also come with clip-art libraries. See for example, **Multimedia Workshop** (CD-ROM for Mac/PC from Ablac).

Special needs

The overlay or concept keyboard is a flexible tool used with special needs and young children. In the Ideas Section you will find many uses in science - but the keyboard requires special programs to make it work. Also, for various needs, there are large and small keyboards, electronic stylus, tiny mice, roller-balls instead of mice, speech devices and switches. Suppliers include The Advisory Unit, Semerc, Cleveland and Resource. **Touch Window** (for PC/Mac/Arc from Resource) is an add-on which substitutes for a mouse in your regular software - you just move a finger on the screen and press. **Windows Concept** (for PC from AU) is a program which makes Windows programs accessible with an overlay keyboard. **Clicker** (Arc/PC/Mac from SEMERC) comes in various flavours allows you to dispense with an overlay keyboard. The 'keyboard' is shown on screen. Recommended.

There are a few outlets for ready-made overlays for the concept keyboard. For example, **Science Simply 1 & 2** (age 8-14, BBC/Arc/PC/Mac from Cleveland) is a selection of overlays to support writing activities in science. These you can use with word processors such as **Folio, Prompt Writer, Stylus, Concept** and **Intercept**. Cd Computing is another supplier.

Resources

Handling information...

Investigations for Key stage 2 (from BECTA and on the Internet) is a pack with good, worked through ideas for handling information in science. **Getting Started with Information handling** (from BECTA) also has worked through activities and several for science. **Science Investigations: an INSET pack for teachers** (from BECTA) is a folder with investigations that generate data they can process with the computer. **IT's primarily science** (Age 8+, from BECTA) is a free and very useful set of leaflets setting out some starting points for using IT in science work. **Data Handling in Primary Science Pack** (for BBC from BECTA) includes a rationale for data handling, a booklet of case studies, sheets with practical ideas as well as a mixture of easy programs. The programs are available separately in the **Information Handling Pack** (for BBC from BECTA). This includes the classic data handling programs **Datashow, Noticeboard, OurFacts, Branch** and the excellent **Sorting Game**.

Primary Data Handling Pack (age 10-12 from The Advisory Unit) has ideas for testing people and their taste buds.

Your choice of data handling software is best driven by a school policy, but here are a few leads: **Junior Pinpoint** (for Archimedes from Logotron) is deservedly popular and very good for surveys. **Clipboard** (age 7-12, PC/Nimbus/Arc from Black Cat Software) is an easy, capable database program. The younger version is **Counter** (age 6-9, PC/Nimbus/Windows from Black Cat Software) and even better **First Workshop** (age 6-9, PC from Black Cat). **Flexidata** (age 9-15, for Nimbus) is capable and it even looks look a Windows program. **Counting Pictures** (age 5-9, PC/Nimbus from Black Cat Software), **PicturePoint** (age 6-9 for Arc from Logotron) and **Pic2gram** (Arc/PC from Cleveland) do pictograms easily. For the easiest of spreadsheet programs see **Number Box** (age 7-13, PC Windows from Black Cat Software).

Key (age 10-15, for PC/Arc/BBC/Nimbus from Anglic) is a database program that is fairly easy yet powerful. A good range of ready-made science datafiles are available for use with it. **KeyNote 2** (for Archimedes from Anglia) is the younger version of the Key database program. There is an easy spreadsheet, **Key Calc** and the younger person's **KeyCount** (age 9-12, for Archimedes from Anglia).

Word processing tools...

You will almost certainly have a word processor, but these writing tools are a bit out of the ordinary, interesting and at risk of being overlooked.

Write Away (age 5-12, PC Windows from Black Cat Software) can be used with different age and ability levels. It is very well tuned to classroom use. **Talking Write Away** speaks the typed text and is also available as an upgrade.

Flexiwrite 3 (age 9-15, for Nimbus) is very capable and makes an old Nimbus look like it is running Word for Windows. **Textease** (age 6-13, PC/Arc from SEMERC) will be a favourite - it talks as you type, you click anywhere on the page to write or draw. Nice feature - on a PC it feels like an Acorn program, and thus a bit strange.

Writer's Toolkit 2 (age 7-11 for Mac from TAG) helps to structure all kinds of writing - this version can turn text to speech. **Thinksheet** (age 7-18 for Arc from TAG) helps to structure and organize ideas graphically, for example it can help sequence information, like a cut-out exercise, on, say, the life cycles. **Intellitalk** (Mac from TAG), **Talking Pendown** (age 4-11 for Archimedes from TAG) and **Talk Write** (Arc from Resource) are talking word processors. **Expression** (Mac from TAG/SCET), a tool to plan, organize and structure ideas as you collect them. It's an interesting tool for building topic webs and preparing talks. Cloze exercises or missing letters and words so often they make for good learning activities - see **Sherlock** (Acorn PC disc from Topologica)

Internet

You can connect your computer to the Internet and get information from the **World Wide Web.** Children can put pages on the Internet to give their work a wide audience. There are special tools in your word processor that do this as easily as writing - and once the page is done you send it, over the phone link, to your Internet service. School service providers include RM, Edex, Argo and Anglia Campus.

You can find software and resources for using computers and science on the author's pages at www.rogerfrost.com

Control technology...

The **First Control Box** (All computers from Philip Harris) is an 8 input and 8 output control box to connect to the Universal Interface from a **First Sense** kit. Uses **First Control software** (All computers from Philip Harris) which is very easy to use - especially the PC Windows version. The software also allows you to build control systems which respond to analogue sensors such as temperature and light sensors.

Contact Controller and **Contact Controller Plus** (PC/ Mac/Arc from Data Harvest) are control boxes in the standard input-output design. The Contact Controller is simpler, having just 4 inputs and 4 outputs compared to the 8 inputs and 8 outputs of Contact Controller Plus. Both connect to the computer using a serial connection so no extras are required. The software is BECTA's Contact which comes in numerous variants.

The **Control Interface** (BBC from Data Harvest) has a standard 8 inputs and 8 outputs and can plug directly into a BBC computer. This can be also be used on PC, Mac and Archimedes machines if it is first plugged into a **Sense and Control** (Data Harvest) interface. The latter allows temperature sensors to be used in your control systems; it uses **Contact software.**

The **Control Box** (BBC/Arc/PC from Commotion) and **The Command Centre** (PC/Arc from Commotion) are two 8 input and 8 output control boxes. These connect to the user or printer port or the serial port respectively and can be controlled by **CoCo** software. **CoCo Plus** (PC/Archimedes from Commotion) is a multitasking control program. It uses 'standard English' to give commands. For example, you enter Switch on Light rather than Sendbit or Switchon on other systems. You click on devices on the screen and words from a control panel and it will say whatever it is asked to do.

Lego First Computer Control (for PC/Mac/Arc from *Lego* suppliers) provides easy control with some analogue sensing capability. The kit is attractive with its own **LOGO software.** The language is fine but is long-winded. The sensing capabilities are almost adequate for primary work . This followed-up *Lego's* black box interface 'A' (BBC/ Nimbus) which uses *Lego's* LOGO control program.It may fall to the wayside now that Lego have **Robolab.** This is like the Mindstorm's intelligent brick which makes control easier than ever. With its data logging add-on it become incredibly powerful-your robot can sense, measure

and do things. Easy and cheap is the stand-alone **Lego control centre** (from TTS) which runs models without a computer.

Deltronics Control-IT (for BBC/Arc/Nimbus with control ports from Deltronics) and the **Deltronics Serial Interface** (for PC/Arc) are two 8 input and 8 output control boxes. These come in several versions, taking jack plugs, banana plugs and a variety of control sensors and accessories. Comes with horrid basic software such as **PC Bits** and **Tron** (Arc).

Discovery (Arc/PC/Mac from Economatics) offers sensing and control features from one box.

For a very inexpensive approach see the **SenSci Control Box** (Arc/PC from Valiant Technology). Valiant's **The Adventures of Hilary** - a package of curriculum materials to go with this will be welcomed too.

Control Accessories

You need devices to plug into the inputs and outputs on the control box. All the control box suppliers offer the necessary input and output bits in various bundles. The output devices include lights, buzzers and motors while the input kits offer light sensors, temperature sensors, pressure mats, reed, push, tilt and light switches. For some unusual projects get a **hydraulic pump** (TTS) and use it to pump water into a tank or water a plant. There is also a ram rod device which has a push-pull action - it might open a 'window' if a greenhouse gets hot. For some challenging work there is even a **Robot Arm** which the children can program to wave hello or perhaps pour a drink (from TTS).

Control Pictures (For all machines from Data Harvest) provide a choice of ready-made control systems - **Traffic Lights**, **House Alarm** and **Washing Machine** scenes. These plug into the standard 8 inputs and 8 outputs control box. They make things easy for beginners - the children use them by writing programs in your control software. Ready-made starter models such as a **Clown**, **Buggy**, **House** or **Traffics lights** are available (Commotion) and these should also plug straight into any control box you have.

First Control Modules (Philip Harris) have been around for ages and take a different approach to control. Each plugs into the Universal Interface of a First Sense kit. The Pelican First Control Module has 5 small coloured lights (LEDs), a buzzer and a push switch mounted on a circuit board. This can simulate a pelican crossing and an alarm system. The Motor Module has a small motor and 2 push switches mounted on a circuit board. It can simulate a cooling fan or a roundabout. The Music Module has a sound device and a push switch and can play the scales or simulate a musical door bell. The Display Module has a seven-segment display - like the numbers in a calculator. The correct segments have to be switched on to display a number so it can be used to simulate the channel indicator on a television. The Dot Matrix Module has a grid of dots which can be turned on and off. It can simulate motorway signs.

Control software

Today there are so many hardware options and machine combinations that it is safer to buy your control software with your control box. You can sometimes use software from one firm with the hardware from another and there is just a chance it will work. There are some third party products too. **Junior Insight** (PC/Mac/Arc from Logotron) has an easy but basic control feature. **Investigate** (PC - from RM) makes it very easy to build elaborate control systems. **Flowol** (age 11-18 for Arc/PC Windows/Mac - Data Harvest) lets you build control systems using a flowchart system - this is fine, but may be daunting at first. **Bits / Nimbits** (for BBC/PC or Nimbus from Northamptonshire) are fairly unrefined control programs. **Tinybits** (Nimbus) from the same people is much more colourful and mouse controlled. Then there is **The Playground** (for Nimbus from Northamptonshire) which is not a control program but a good introduction to one. In this graphical, pre-LOGO program children use the mouse to create a sequence of actions for a Teddy character. It is not so much a science program but worth a look for the control.

Robots...

Pixie (Swallow Systems) is a simple and small programmable floor robot. Uses rechargeable NiCad batteries, a small keyboard and can remember programs, even when switched off. It can be programmed to ride on play mats with letters, numbers or farmyard scenery.

Pip (Swallow Systems) is a well established robot with a 24 key membrane keyboard. You can program it to move forward, turn, make a sound, or go backwards. Sensors such as a light sensor, a bump sensor or a magnet sensor can be attached so that Pip can be made to change its direction when it bumps into an object. It can connect to a computer for use with **LogoWriter** (PC) or **PipNim** (PC/Nimbus) software. It looks best when dressed-up as a lorry or animal.

The **Valiant Control Console** (Valiant) is a stand-alone controller keypad which saves you having to use a computer. You plug your model into the console and then use the keypad to enter commands. The console can remember procedures (sub-programs) which you can assemble in a larger program.

The **Valiant Turtle** (BBC/Arc/PC/Nimbus from Valiant) is the original remote controlled turtle which responds to Logo commands from the computer. Plenty of scope for fun with Logo variants such as WinLogo, Logotron Logo, PC Logo and LogoWriter.

The Valiant Roamer is a Smartie-shaped robot with a keypad. It can be programmed to follow a route. Accessories, such as basic sensors, trail pens and fix-on jackets are available. A computer interface (BBC/Nimbus/Arc/PC from Valiant) and software allows you to store Roamer programs on disc while a control box allows you to use the Roamer keypad to write control programs.

The **Lego Dacta Control Centre** (from *Lego* suppliers) can control three output devices, such as a light and motor on a Lego model, using a simple keypad. It works independently of the computer and can learn sequences of actions and replay them repeatedly. However Lego's **Robolab**, mentioned earlier, is more the object of desire.

Sensor kits...

Live (for PC/Arc from Griffin, Research Machines, Curriculum Warehouse or Logotron) is a junior version of the LogIT device used in secondary schools. The basic kit comes with carrying case, computer cable, Live box, a temperature sensor, light sensor and sound sensor - all you need except the software. You can then choose your preferred software from **Junior Insight**, **Insight** or **Investigate**, described below. There is an accessory pack with useful sensors: two light switches for timing events, a handy extension cable and another temperature sensor to help you compare readings between say, cooling cups of tea. One other device included is an LED - which you can switch on or off in a simple control system.

A good range of other sensors are available to use with **Live** (from Griffin). These allow you to measure pressure, breathing, air humidity, position and more. Useful is the **CheckIT** clip-on display unit that allows you to see readings away from the computer. So too is the connecting kit which gets the Live system working with palmtop computers.

Discovery (Arc/PC/Mac from Economatics) is a control and sensing kit with a variety of options. It uses **Discover Sensing** software.

Ecolog (from Data Harvest) is a budged priced device that takes reading from built-in sensors though extra plug in sensors are available. Also takes readings away from the computer and works with Sensing Science software.

First Sense (PC/Mac/Arc/BBC/ Nimbus from Philip Harris) has a designed look to it. The sensors are automatically recognised when you start the software. **First Sense software** is simple and versions for older computers (eg Nimbus/BBC) are overshadowed by versions for today's computers. You can add control accessories and extra sensors to the kit. The starter kit consists of a computer cable, temperature sensor, light sensor, sound sensor, software and a Universal interface. Then there are options: **Datadisc Explore** software (age 11-15, for PC from Philip Harris) is a much more capable alternative to First Sense software. A second temperature sensor is worth having to compare temperatures for example, one can be indoors and one outdoors. Many other sensors are available.

RM Detector (RM Window Box PC from RM) possibly the cheapest of all the logging systems - this uses the computer sound card to capture approximate temperature and light level information. The graphs, appear within Microsoft Excel.

Extra Sense (for PC/Arc from Deltronics) and **Sense-IT** (for BBC/Arc/Nimbus from Deltronics) are used in secondary schools and you make up your kit depending upon what you need. There are sensors for temperature, light and sound as well as light gates or light switches for timing events. Extra Sense comes with software but also works with Insight or Junior Insight software. Sense-IT uses Leicester Toolkit software (Deltronics) which is easy, basic but adequate.

Sense (for BBC/Nimbus/Arc with analogue port from Data Harvest or TTS) is a basic kit with software, temperature sensors, light sensor and a pressure mat for timing. This provides an adequate system although sensors are not automatically recognised. Some quite special software is now (1996) available for this.

SensorBox (for BBC/Arc with analogue port from Commotion) is a basic kit with software, temperature sensors, light sensor and sound sensor. This provides a reasonable system and on the Archimedes uses the easy CoSe software.

Stopwatch Pro (for Archimedes with analogue port from Commotion) allows you to time fast events, such as a moving buggy. It consists of a pair of light gates and software. **Time IT** (for BBC/Arc with analogue or serial port from Commotion) does similar but using two floor trip-switches and different software.

The **Panthera measuring box** (for BBC - Panthera) is a simple and low priced unit with sensors for temperature, light and sound. Rather limited but fine for work on BBC computers.

Some sensor kits have the additional facility to take sense readings away from the computer. You could take the sensors out of doors and monitor the weather, noise pollution and so on. This is a useful feature, but the extra expense makes it less of a priority at this level. The following kits are aimed at secondary schools, but middle schools should find them of interest:

LogIT Datameter 1000 (Griffin) is a compact device with a built-in screen, a green start button and a red stop button. Like the **Live** box above it uses the same LogIT sensors - which there are many in the range. Those who have the older LogIT device can benefit from the **CheckIT** display unit - showing readings and additional information on a small screen. These all work with Junior Insight, Insight and Investigate. Each can perform control using accessories such as **AlarmIT** (Griffin).

EasyLog Sense & Control (Data Harvest) has a remote facility too. It works with Junior Insight, Insight, Investigate, Sensing Science and Practical Science software. Also works with **PriSM** software on Archimedes computers. Most control boxes can be connected directly to it.

The **DLplus** (Philip Harris) uses First Sense sensors and has a screen which helps when you want to see readings from the sensors. The keyboard and menu make it easy to use away from the computer.

Discovery (Arc/PC/Mac from Economatics) comes as a remote logger.

Weather stations which are specially designed for long term monitoring are also available (from AU, MJP).

Sensor software...

All the sensor suppliers should be able to supply you with a full kit of sensors and software. You can get software which works with your kit from third parties too.

Investigate! (for PC Windows from Research Machines) was developed at Homerton College and supports most sensor kits that work on the PC. It offers a choice of ways to see your measurements - such as a bar gauge, a time graph, a number and it will even speak its readings. It can control devices using a control box connected to the data logging interface and it does so easily. Still ahead of its time. A booklet and video is available called **'Investigate'** **data logging in the primary school** - from SCIcentre - the National Centre for Initial Teacher Training in Primary Science (address on page 123)

Junior Insight (for PC Windows/Arc/Mac from Logotron) was developed at Leicester University and supports most sensor kits that plug into modern computers. Uses a simple start button to start recording as well as some tools that let you take readings from the graph. A second program is part of the package and allows you to time events if you have light switches or light gate sensors. Middle schools should also look at Insight - a version for older children.

Sensing Science (age 8-11 from Data Harvest) has displays - a bar, a digital reading, a meter with a needle and a time graph. A 'snapshot' feature takes one-off readings and shows these as a table or series of bars. A nice, if brilliant feature lets children record for up to a minute and pause the display as they draw and predict where the graph line will go next. The software works only with Data Harvest equipment including Sense & Control, **EcoLog** and **Easy Sense** (Disc for Acorn/Mac/PC from Data Harvest)

PriSM (BBC/Arc fitted with an analogue port - from Data Harvest) is a capable piece of software with a good range of display styles such as bar, gauge and time graph. It is straightforward to use, and while it cannot recognise the sensors you connect, it works with many 'analogue port' sensor kits. There is an enhanced version for the Archimedes which has control features.

Science Measurement Toolkit (Version 5 for BBC/Arc/Nimbus fitted with an analogue port - from Leicester) is an inexpensive suite of data logging programs. It can count events and can be set to start-up with an easy menu..

Sundries

Computer companies include Apple Xemplar, Compaq, Dell, IBM, ICL Fujitsu and RM.

Cables and connectors in all forms - Videk Ltd

Glossary

Branching Database - a special kind of database. It allows you to build an identification key to sort out a set of animals, plants and so on. A branching database on animals asks you questions about an animal and will identify it for you. Using a branching database encourages observation and discussion.

CD-ROM - a computer disc which looks like a compact music disc. However, instead of music the disc stores text, photos, moving images and sounds. You place the disc in a CD-ROM player and see the images on the screen. An incredible amount of information - an entire encyclopaedia can be stored on one compact disc. Children can search it to explore a topic. Often there is a measure of interaction and this, of course, is a good starting point for something educational. CD-ROM is like all software - not always wonderful. CD-Interactive is another technology with excellent potential.

Concept keyboard or Overlay keyboard - is an alternative to a button-type keyboard. The keyboard is an A4 or A3 sized tablet which plugs into the computer though wireless versions are available. Onto this you place a sheet of paper, called an overlay. The overlay has words, pictures or even objects on it. When say, a picture is pressed the screen displays some words. This tool can make computing more accessible to pupils - especially younger ones and those with special needs.

Control technology - allows you to control a motorised device, such as a fan, with the computer. Using sensors you might arrange for the fan to switch on and off as the temperature changes. Control technology develops problem solving and computer programming skills. It is an aid to understanding how things work. Control technology has some applications in science teaching.

Database program - a program which lets you store data - such as the data you collect in a survey. You set up a series of headings under which you enter your survey results. You can search, sort, graph or print the data. You might search a database of people, to find those with dark hair and brown eyes.

Datafile - another word for a database, or collection of information about one topic.

Data logging - a method of logging or collecting data from sensors. Strictly speaking, data logging uses devices, called data loggers, which you can take away from the computer and collect readings in the field.

Desk-top publisher - a program to assemble a page with text, borders, boxes and pictures. The text is prepared in a word processor, the pictures in a graphics program. A DTP program can really help produce quite attractive work. Modern word processors have many of the features of DTP programs and are adequate in most cases. A DTP program would need to be special to have beside a good word processor.

Digital camera - uses magnetic media instead of film. These are the ultimate instant-print cameras and many times more useful. Worth considering if you use cameras as a recording tool in your teaching.

Drawing program - a kind of graphics program where each item on the screen is an object you can scale, move or modify. These are the best choice of program for drawing diagrams. See also Painting program.

Graphics programs - these use the computer screen as an electronic canvas. It's very easy to erase mistakes, which helps those who cannot draw. There are also special features which have no comparison - such as painting with striped paint, copying areas, flipping areas upside down or changing their size. Pictures can be pasted into reports, posters and newspapers.

Multimedia - technology which allows you to experience words, sounds, pictures, animation and/or video when you use the computer. With a modern computer, you can assemble such media yourself to create your own multimedia presentations. A major growth industry with potential for learning about science.

Modelling - a way of representing real-life on the computer. You can experiment with a model and find out how things affect it. A spreadsheet can be used to create a mathematical model of how much water we use in a day. There are science-based programs which make modelling more accessible.

Internet - a world-wide network of computers that allows you to communicate with schools and anyone else on the system. You can also browse through and interact with pages of information called Web pages. You need a modem to link the computer to the phone line. You also need to subscribe to a service (such as CampusWorld or RM's Eduweb). Neither of these are expensive, the main costs are for the phone calls.

Painting program - a kind of graphics program where you paint on the screen. These are the best choice of program for working with 'art' and photographs. See also Drawing program.

Printers - there are many different printer technologies in circulation. The dot-matrix and daisy-wheel printers are pretty-much history now. Ink-jet printers are cheap to buy and do a good black. Colour versions are worth having. Everyone should have access to a laser printer - a photocopier-quality printer.

Robots - devices which can be programmed to follow directions, draw a trace on the floor or follow a light source. Some of these work independently of the computer, some can be remote-controlled by the computer.

Scanner - an accessory which allows you to capture pictures or photographs for the computer screen. The picture can then be re-sized and printed alongside the text in a worksheet. An exciting, easy and affordable tool which is well worth a look.

Sensors - there are sensors to measure physical quantities such as temperature, light or sound. Measurements are shown on a computer screen as a number or graph.

Simulation - a program written to simulate real-life. For example, 'At home in Wattville' is a simulation which shows the use of electricity in the home. You can switch appliances on and off and see the effect on the electricity bill.

Spreadsheet - a program that handles data in a table. The data can also be sorted and graphed. Spreadsheets are valuable for handling results from investigations.

Word processor - a program for drafting, improving and printing written work. Many word processors allow you to change the type style or even add pictures to your work.

Addresses

For updates of this list, see the Internet pages at www.rogerfrost.com

4Mation Educational Resources, Linden Lea, Rock Park, Devon, EX32 9AQ. Tel: 01271 45566

Ablac Learning Works, South Devon House, Newton Abbot, Devon, TQ12 2BP. Telephone: 01626 332233 Fax: 01626 331464

Anglia Multimedia, SCA, PO Box 18, Benfleet, Essex SS7 1AZ Telephone: 01268 755811

Appian Way Software, Old Co-Operative Buildings, Langley Park, Durham DH7 9XE. Tel: 0191 373 1389

Association for Science Education, College Lane, Hatfield. AL10 9AA. Telephone: 01707 267411 Fax: 01707 266532

Attica Cybernetics, Unit 2, Kings Meadow, Ferry Hinksey Road, Oxford, OX2 0DP. Telephone: 01865 791346 Fax: 01865 794561

AVP, School Hill Centre, Chepstow, Gwent, NP6 5PH. Telephone: 01291 625439

BECTA, Milburn Hill Road, Science Park, Coventry CV4 7JJ. Telephone: 01203 416994 Fax: 01203 411418

Black Cat Educational Software, The Barns, Tir-y-Graig Isaf, Cwm Camlais, Nr Brecon, Powys. Telephone: 01874 636835

British Library, Publications, 41 Russell Square, London WC1B 3DG. Telephone: 0207 412 7535 Fax: 0207 412 7768

British Gas Education, PO Box 70, Wetherby, West Yorks. Tel: 01937 843141

BT Education Services, 81 Newgate Street, London EC1 7AJ. Telephone: 0800 622303.

BTL Publishing, Business and Innovation Centre, Angel Way, Listerhills, Bradford, BD7 1BX. Telephone: 01274 841320 Fax: 01274 841348

Cambridgeshire Software House (CSH), The Town Hall, St Ives, Huntingdon, Cambridgeshire, PE17 4AL. Tel: 01480 66805

Cd Computing, (Concept keyboard overlays), Thorpe Lea, Greenacres, Rawmarsh, Rotherham, S62 6LD. Tel: 01709 526833

Cleveland Educational Computing Centre (CECC), Prissick Base, Marton Road, Middlesborough, Cleveland. TS4 3RZ. Telephone: 01642 325417.

Curriculum Warehouse / Commotion, Unit 11, Tannery Road, Tonbridge, Kent, TN9 1RF Telephone: 01732 773399

Creative Curriculum Software, 5 Clover Hill Road, Saville Park, Halifax, HX1 2YG. Telephone: 01422 340524

Data Harvest, Woburn Lodge, Waterloo Road, Linslade, Leighton Buzzard, Beds., LU7 7NR. Telephone: 01525 373666 Fax: 01525 851638

Deltronics, Church Road Industrial Estate, Gorslas, Llanelli, Dyfed, SA14 7NF Telephone: 01269 843728 Fax: 01269 845527

Dorling Kindersley Family Library, 1 Horsham Gates, North Street, Horsham, West Sussex, RH13 5PJ. Telephone: 01403 270274 Fax: 01403 274476

Economatics, Epic House, Darnall Road, Sheffield, S9 5AA. Telephone: 0114 256 1122 Fax: 0114 243 9306

Education Interactive, Hinton House, Hinton, Dorset, BH23 7EA. Telephone: 01425 272235 Fax: 01425 273784

Educational Electronics - see Data Harvest

ESM, Abbeygate House, East Road, Cambridge, CB1 1DB. Telephone: 01223 357788 Fax: 01223 460557

Flexible Software, PO Box 100, Abingdon, Oxon, OX13 6PQ. Telephone: 01865 391148

Griffin & George, Bishop Meadow Road, Loughborough, Leics., LE11 0RG. Telephone: 01509 233344

Granada Learning - See SEMERC

Hampshire Microtechnology Centre, Connaught Lane, Paulsgrove, Portsmouth, PO6 4SJ. Telephone: 01705 378266 Fax: 01705 379443

IT in Science/Roger Frost 7 Sutton Place, London E9 6EH. Telephone/Fax: 0208 986 3526 www.rogerfrost.com

KimTec UK, Fairways House, 8 Highland Road, Colehill, Dorset, BH21 2QN

Koch Media Ltd, East Street, Farnham, Surrey, GU9 7XX. Telephone: 01252 714340 Fax: 01252 711121

Kudlian Soft, 8 Barrow Road, Kenilworth, Warwickshire, CV8 1EH. Telephone/Fax: 01926 851147

Leicester University, School of Education, 21 University Road, Leicester, LE1 7RF. Telephone: 01162 523656

Logotron, 124 Cambridge Science Park, Milton Road, Cambridge. Telephone: 01223 425558 Fax: 01223 425349

Macademic, Trams Ltd, 55-55 Wlton Road, London SW1V 1DE. Telephone: 0207 630 6844 Fax: 0207 233 8489

Mail Order suppliers include AVP Education Interactive, Schools Direct CD, TAG, Kimtec

MAPE (Micros in Primary Education) c/o The Old Vicarage, Skegby Road, Normanton-on-Trent, Notts. NG23 6BR

Microscope, Centre for Science Education, Sheffield Hallam University, Collegiate Crescent Campus, Sheffield, S10 1BP. Telephone: 0114 253 2209 Fax: 0114 253 2299

MJP-Geopacks, Box 23, St Just, Cornwall, TR19 7JS. Telephone: 01736 787808 Fax: 01736 787880

Initial Teacher Training in Primary Science, SCIcentre, School of Education, 21 University Road, Leicester LE1 7RF Tel 0115 252 3659 Fax 0116 252 3653

New Vision, Cumberland House, 80 Scrubbs Lane, London NW10 6AH. Telephone: 0208 964 3334 Fax: 0208 964 5424.

Northamptonshire Computer Centre, Barry Road, Northampton, NN1 5JS. Telephone: 01604 241090

Oxford Computer Education, Wheatley Centre, Littleworth Road, Oxford OX33 1PH

Panthera, 5 Cedar Avenue, Beeston, Nottingham, NG9 2HA. Telephone: 0602 256309

Research Machines, New Mill House, Milton Park, Abingdon, Oxon, OX14 4BR. Telephone: 01235 826868

Resource, 51 High Street, Kegworth, Derby, DE74 2DA. Telephone: 01509 672222

Rickitt Educational Media, Great Western House, Langport, Somerset, TA10 9YU. Telephone: 01458 253636 Fax: 01458 253646

Schools Direct CD, The Green, Ravensthorpe, Northampton. NN6 8EP. Telephone: 01604 770099 Fax: 01604 770702

Semerc/Granada Learning, 1 Broadbent Road, Watersheddings, Oldham, OL1 4LB Telephone: 0161 627 4469 Fax: 0161 627 2381

Sherston Software, Angel House, High Street, Sherston, Malmesbury, Wilts. SN16 0LH. Telephone: 01666 840433

SITSS, Shropshire IT support service, Bourne House, Radbrook, Shrewsbury, SY3 9BJ. Telephone:: 0743 246043 Fax: 0743 368481

Soft Teach Educational, Sturgess Farmhouse, Longbridge Deverill, Wilts BA12 7EA Tel 01985 840 329 Fax 01985 840 331 http://www.soft-teach.demon.co.uk/
SPA, PO Box 59, Tewsbury, Glos GL20 6AB. Telephone: 01684 81700

Storm Educational Software, Digby Road, Sherborne, Dorset, DT9 3NN. Telephone/Fax: 01935 817699

Swallow Systems, 134 Cock Lane, High Wycombe, Bucks. HP13 7EA. Telephone: 01494 813471 Fax 01494 813552

TAG Developments, 19 High Street, Gravesend, Kent, DA11 0BA. Telephone: 0800 591 262

Advisory Unit (AU), Computers in Education, 126 Great North Road, Hatfield, Herts, AL9 5JZ. Telephone: 01707 266714. Fax: 01707 273684

Topologica Software, 1 South Harbour, Harbour Village, Penryn, Cornwall, TR10 8LR. Tel: 01326 377771 Fax: 01326 376755

TTS, Technology Teaching Systems, Unit 7, Monk Road, Alfreton, Derbyshire, D55 7RL Tel: 01773 830255 Fax: 01773 830325

Understanding Electricity, The Electricity Association, 30 Millbank, London, SW1P 4RD. Telephone: 0207 344 5839

Unilab Ltd, The Science Park, Hutton Street, Blackburn, Lancs., BB1 3BT. Telephone: 01254 681222 Fax: 01254 681777

Valiant Technology, Myrtle House, 69 Salcott Road, London SW11 6DQ. Tel: 0207 924 2366 Fax: 0207 924 1892

Videk Ltd, Unit 10, Bowman Trading Estate, Westmoreland Road, London NW9 9RW. Telephone: 0208 204 6690

YITM - see Granada Learning / SEMERC

Index

Resources

Section
4